HOW TO MAKE MONEY ONLINE IN 2023

A BEGINNER'S GUIDE TO ALMOST PASSIVE INCOME WITH ECOMMERCE, AFFILIATE MARKETING, SELF-PUBLISHING, NICHE WEBSITES, ONLINE COURSES AND MORE

MICHAEL WU

CONTENTS

INTRODUCTION

There's never been a better time to start an online business.

When the pandemic hit, people were increasingly turning to the Internet to find either a way to make a living, or a way to pivot their existing businesses and build an online presence around them.

This book is written for those who belong to either of the two camps — but most importantly, for those who want to earn enough money online to support themselves financially while accessing more and more wealth and freedom in their lives.

And there truly is room for more wealth to be acquired through the Internet. No matter how rife with competition and convolution every online industry seems to be these days, there are always opportunities to be had.

New ideas and products can still make a huge impact. Startups and small businesses can still thrive. They don't get lost in the Internet jungle…if you know what you're doing.

If you've picked up this book, you *won't* get lost because I'll be guiding you through those very first, small but essential, steps. More specifically, I will help you:

1. Get acquainted with the world of online business
2. Gain a foundational understanding of branding and marketing
3. Get an insider look at the most profitable online business models and sub-models
4. Figure out the type of online business that suits you best
5. Equip yourself with the necessary tools and resources to get started in the online business of your choice

Are you ready to make this radical, lifechanging move? If so, I welcome you to this exciting new journey in your life.

- *Michael Wu*
Author

1

THE BASICS OF ONLINE BUSINESS

Online businesses are booming – and they will continue to do so for years to come. Due to our current era of digitalization, being online is no longer an option. It's a necessity.

But why are some online business owners making it big time while others are constantly hustling and struggling?

The answer is simple: **You can't go about an online business blindly**. You have to have solid knowledge of what you are doing and put a plan into place based on that knowledge. There's simply no room for "let's try this and see how it goes". No. You need to know what you're doing, how to be strategic about it, and also put in the legwork.

If you can access a mentor – or even a book like this – you will be doing yourself a major favor and avoiding most of the pitfalls you would have otherwise been oblivious to.

THE BENEFITS OF ONLINE BUSINESS

Owning an online business, regardless of what model you follow, is proven to have the following benefits:

✔ Low operating costs

It goes without saying that you will not need to worry about paying salaries, benefits, warehouses, office/shop rent and the excessive overhead that come with a brick-and-mortar business. And you can even completely avoid purchasing inventory depending on the business model you select.

✔ 24/7 availability

Online businesses do not have a "Sorry, we're closed" sign (unless you have a customer support line which operates during certain hours of the day). That means your site or shop is always open, and orders are constantly rolling in.

✔ **Work whenever and wherever you want**

When it comes to online business, you can literally work in your pajamas at your bed-office, or wearing sweatpants on a deck chair out in the garden, or even in your swimsuit at some remote beach. You can also work *whenever* you want, as you make your own rules and schedule.

✔ **Unlimited global reach**

You may own a smalltown business, but once it's online its reach becomes limitless. Now you can access the world, receive orders both locally and overseas, and expand your brand's reach and scaling potential.

✔ **Faster delivery of products or services**

When you're operating an online business with little to no inventory, you don't have to leave your desk in the middle of the day to run errands and send off orders. Nor will your customers have to wait 'til you're open to ask about a refund or report a faulty item. Every interaction is an email away!

✔ More eco-friendly

Forget the paper shredder and the constant waste that gathers when you have a typical brick-and-mortar business. When you have an online business, almost all of your paperwork is digitalized.

✔ Improved customer support

Customers don't have to wait until opening hours to get a hold of you. Emails work wonders – and if you're not always there to answer, you can simply set up a chatbot to handle things for you in your absence.

As you can see the benefits are endless... But what's more exciting about online business is the opportunity to turn it into a passive income stream.

THE TRUTH ABOUT PASSIVE INCOME

You may have come across the term "passive income" before, but might not have fully grasped its meaning. Fret not, because I have you covered here.

Passive income is earnings received from businesses and ventures you are not actively involved with.

For example, if you're investing in stocks or leasing real estate to someone, you simply sit back and let the money come to you. You don't "work" to earn it (but you did make an investment once).

Similarly, passive income can be applied to the online business world.

But what kind of businesses fare well when it comes to passive income? The most commonly utilized models are:

- **E-commerce businesses** where manufacturing, warehousing and shipping is not required on your behalf (i.e., the *dropshipping* model).
- **Digital products** that are made by/for you once, yet make earnings for years to come (i.e., *eBooks* and *online courses*).
- **Service businesses** that are automated thanks to systems and teams that work for you (i.e., a creative *freelance agency*).

Needless to say, not all businesses can function as passive income streams. Some may apply to more of a **semi-passive income** structure, while others may require a lot more input from you, in which case they do not qualify as passive income at all.

But why is passive income so important in the first place? The answer lies in the reasons one may want to pursue it:

- More freedom (most passive income enthusiasts like to travel the world as "digital nomads" or spend more time with their families)
- Higher earnings with fewer to non-existent work hours
- Change of lifestyle and the way you work
- The remote/home-based work setting
- Early retirement
- Stress reduction
- Personalized schedule
- Scalability potential
- Digitalization of the business
- Outsouring work rather than doing it yourself
- Diversity of projects and opportunities
- Access to a global audience
- Multiple ways to sell one product/service

Despite the multiple benefits and plausible reasons you may have for pursuing passive income, there are some **harsh truths** when it comes to this business approach:

1. Passive income is not a get-rich-quick scheme.
2. Instead, it requires time and effort, particularly during the initial start-up phase.
3. Automation tools and systems can make a business more passive, but you have to set these processes up, hire and train a team, etc.
4. Semi-passive income businesses will require your presence, if not your direct work, every so often.
5. A passive income business does not guarantee early retirement. In fact, nothing is guaranteed.
6. Passive income cannot be predicted in earnings and numbers (no matter what some gurus may claim); but proven strategies can be followed and emulated.
7. Passive income does not mean you will be 100% carefree. You are still a business owner running a business, managing operations and finances, keeping up with taxes, etc.

If you're still here and undiscouraged by the reality of things, then I congratulate you! You are most likely the material passive income business owners are made of.

But what should your business even be selling online to make the most of that passive income?

SELLING PRODUCTS VS SERVICES ONLINE

Should you sell tangible products or services through your online business? The decision may be tougher than you think.

First, let's start by defining each:

Tangible Product: A measurable, touchable, visible product that can be packaged and shipped to the buyer.

Service: An intangible product which requires interaction with the buyer.

Tangible products are items that can be shipped from one place to another and delivered to one's doorstep. They can be tech gadgets, homewares, gym equipment, vitamins, food, TVs, phones, fishing gear, paper goods, art, jewelry, e-cigarettes and basically anything you can hold in your hands or touch.

- **Where to sell:** Amazon, Shopify and eBay are

the top platforms used for selling tangible products.

Services can be offered either face-to-face or via the Internet - we will deal mostly with the latter in this book. These services can be online language lessons, coaching sessions, marketing consultations, freelance tasks like writing or designing, and so much more.

- ➢ **Where to sell:** You can sell eBooks via Amazon, audiobooks via ACX, creative and consultive services via freelancing sites like Upwork, professional services via directories, or any kind of service via your own website.

Here are some truths to wrap your mind around before opting to offer a tangible product or a service:

Tangible products require the following...	Services require the following...
Manufacturing Who is making these products and how would you acquire them? What are the costs?	***A provider*** Are you providing the service directly to the client? If not, who is?
Inventory Who is storing the products?	***No inventory***
An ordering system Who is handling the orders, picking, packing and shipping the products?	***A booking system*** How can prospective clients book your service? How can such a system/tool be set up and who will manage it?
An accessible platform How are these products being sold? How can customers access them or get to know about them?	***An accessible platform*** How will your prospective clients purchase these services? What tools will be used to offer the service?
A team How much work can you do on your own? Which departments would you require help with?	***A team*** How much work can you do on your own? Which departments would you require help with?
Passive income Can you automate the process from picking the order to packaging and shipping it without lifting a finger? Can automation tools or a team handle all processes for you?	***Semi-passive income (through outsourcing)*** A service is an interaction, which equals to visible work being done. You may, however, be able to create a semi-passive income service business if you outsource the service deliverables (have a representative, freelancer or employee deliver the service to the client).
Sales and earnings Are you selling the products for a full profit or are you simply making a commission? How much will you be earning per product sold?	***Earnings, time and interaction*** Are you charging for time spent or per service purchased? And how will you carry out that interaction?

And let's now introduce a different kind of product: the **digital product or info-product**:

Digital Product: An intangible digitalized product that is downloadable, possibly printable, and accessible via an online platform (membership site, online library, course platform, etc).

Digital products take the form of eBooks, digital reports, courses, and anything that can be viewed on a screen.

Here is some more information on digital products:

Digital products or info-products require the following...
At least one digitalized product Who will create it? What are the costs entailed in creating it (you might need a designer, writer, coder, etc)?
No inventory
An accessible platform How will your prospective customers purchase your digital product? How will it be accessed and/or downloaded?
A team How much work can you do on your own? Which departments would you require help with?
Semi-passive income (through systems) If you aren't selling a product like an eBook through Amazon, you can create automated systems and processes for the ordering and downloading/delivery or your digital product on your own website.
Sales and pricing How will your product be priced? Will it be part of a bigger group of products (like a course or digital package)?

Now, you may already be getting excited about the plethora of options you have available here. But you can't get started and actually be *successful* without first considering your niche.

HOW TO PICK AN INDUSTRY OR NICHE

Picking an industry or *niche* is a pivotal step before venturing into any new business. When it comes to starting an online business and braving the big bad wolf known as the Internet, choosing a niche is probably the most important decision you will ever make.

The Merriam-Webster dictionary defines a *niche* as follows:

> **Niche** is a place, employment, status, or activity for which a person or thing is best fitted.

Sounds simple, right? Wrong. You'd be surprised how many new business owners think a niche is simply a broad industry they can elect to be a part of.

This is where the term **niche market** comes in. A niche market is not a broad or overly generic thing. It's more of a subset or segment within an industry that exhibits specific features, deals with specific products or services, and applies to a sub-group of customer characteristics.

For example, let's assume you sell tangible products. Your industry may be tech gadgets, but your niche market is smartphones. And you can get more specific still, like focusing only on a particular smartphone brand, like iPhones.

The same can apply to services. Your industry may be freelance writing but your niche market is copywriting. And to hone in even more, maybe you write only landing page copy, or your copy is addressed towards a particular kind of client, like wellness practitioners located in Syndey Australia.

And the same can be said for digital products. Your industry may be coaching, but your niche is corporate coaching for Canadian CEOs. Spiral deeper into the niche and you may choose to specialize in corporate coaching specifically for Canadian CEOs who are female SaaS founders.

And here's the secret: the more you drill into that "dot" and narrow down your offering, the easier it will become to market yourself and stand out among your competitors.

But how do you got about picking the industry that suits you best? I would recommend you follow these five steps:

1. Choose a niche you are passionate about.

Imagine spending days, weeks, months, even years on setting up and scaling a business that deals with a product or service you aren't even interested in. Don't go for what seems profitable, but rather start with something you are passionate about or at least interested in. If you need to, go through lists of niches and see which speaks to you. Or maybe you already know…

2. Make sure you are at least somewhat familiar with this niche (or a willing to learn a lot about it).

Being familiar with the niche at hand will save you time and energy on learning the nuts and bolts. And being "familiar" doesn't mean you have to be an expert or hold a PhD on the subject. For example, maybe you once worked in a health store and enjoy keeping fit and healthy — in this case, selling supplements may be a good niche for you. To boost your confidence, you can always take a cheap online course and learn more about your given topic.

3. Compare your chosen niche to your personality.

It may be a disillusioning experience, but you will have to ask yourself if you're truly cut out for the niche you've selected. For instance, if you want to sell coaching services but are too shy to get on camera, maybe you should consider a different type of product/service, like eBooks or coaching via email. Make a list of the various ways you can sell your idea without it impinging on your personality.

4. Research, research, research!

Research is key to grasping where you stand as a business among a crowded market and who you're up against. Who are you addressing via your product/service (target audience)? What are this person's needs and how can you fulfill them? Who else is offering a similar or identical product/service to yours? Why are they successful and where do they lack? Can you fill that gap? And how can your product/service be better or different? Once you have these questions answered, you are on your way to making your online business a reality.

5. Test and evaluate your niche

There is no way to know from the onset how profitable your niche will be (again, ignore the gurus). Therefore, the best option is to test your idea before you officially launch it. You can do this by setting up a cheaper blog versus a full-blown website, writing a shorter book, selling very few products, and generally testing the waters before you plunge into the deep end.

Once you have selected and tested your niche and garnered positive results, it's time to start building your brand.

BUILDING YOUR BRAND

Branding is something many people understand wrongly. For most, it translates to a logo, maybe even a color palette and a business card. But branding goes far beyond design. It also includes elements like language, tone of voice, product/offering, ethos, mission and marketing strategy.

So, let's start with the definition of *branding*, not based on the dictionary interpretation, but in the words of one of the most prolific businessmen of all time, Amazon's own Jeff Bezos:

"Your brand is what other people say about you when you're not in the room."

Think about how you react about the brands you enjoy the most. How about your favorite deodorant or shampoo? What entices you to keep buying this product? Is it the quality? The price? The fact that it is cruelty-free or naturally derived? It's most likely *not* about the colors or logo, that's for sure!

What do you tell your friends about this product? How do you talk about it? Do you recommend it? Do you recall all its features? This is what Jeff Bezos is talking about.

As a new online business, you will need to question how you too can be someone's "favorite" or go-to product/service. Ask yourself the following questions:

- Who will my brand be serving? (This is your **Target Audience**)
- How can I serve this ideal customer in the best way possible *or* how can I make my brand unique? (Otherwise known as your **Unique Selling Point**)
- How can I make my brand memorable? (What will customers remember and remark about?)

- How can I pull ahead of my competitors? (Keep in mind, you may be competing against big or even giant brands here)

There is no need to have the perfect answers just yet – but a general grasp of who you are serving and how you will be doing so is necessary. Your brand will mold itself out of continuous trial and error and constant testing until you get it juuust right. No brand is immaculate from the get-go.

Are you ready to get started with the actual brand-building process now? Here are three steps to jump-starting your brand:

1. Brand Strategy
2. Brand Identity
3. Brand Marketing

1. Brand Strategy

This is where you will define your brand, its target customers, and its unique selling point. It's those very first questions we discussed earlier. It should also include competitor research and defining your brand voice and mission. Working with a strategist or copywriter is usually worthwhile at this stage.

2. Brand Identity

This is where design comes in. You should create your logo, design a color palette, you're your fonts, and any other elements (icons, packaging, web design) that will accompany your brand. Needless to say, you will ideally be working with a graphic and web designer during these stages.

3. Brand Marketing

As the heading suggests, this is the marketing phase (do keep in mind, though, that marketing is a continuous process). Marketing is your packaging if you sell tangible products, your ads, SEO content, website copy, emails, social media, and anything else you plan to utilize for the purpose of making sales. A marketing expert or agency may be able to assist with several or even all of these aspects. We'll get more into marketing in the next two sub-chapters.

IT'S ALL ABOUT THE LIST

I'm going to put some extra emphasis on email list-building, as email is still one of the most powerful, impactful and lucrative forms of digital marketing: For every dollar spent on email marketing, you can expect about a **3800% return** – and that's *not* an exaggeration.

But let's begin with a definition of *email lists*:

> An **email list** is a collection of emails that you have received through your website and intend to make use of for your marketing and engagement efforts.
>
> This is also known as a *subscriber's list.*

If you've ever subscribed to a weekly newsletter via a brand's website or opted to receive a freebie like an eBook by typing your name and email into a form, then you have become a "**lead**" and subscriber to that email list.

Here are some **further stats and advantages** to convince you of how powerful email marketing is:

- 99% of people check their emails every day, so you're accessing nearly every single one of your subscribers.
- You have 100% control over your email list and its contents; no one can take them away from you.

- Emails can be personalized. You can gather more than just a subscriber's email (like names, genders, locations, ages and birthdays).
- Emails can be segmented based on your audience, their ages, location, preferences, etc. Marketers who use segmented campaigns note as much as a 760% increase in revenue!
- You can collect reviews, ratings and feedback from your subscribers through polls and surveys.
- You can directly communicate with your audience at any given time. This is a great way to instill trust in your brand and grow your brand-customer relationships.
- Email marketing campaigns send traffic to your website for no cost.
- You can direct your subscribers anywhere you want; be it a specific product page on your website, a giveaway form, even a partner website.

So how does one even get started with email marketing and "building a list"? If you're adamant about growing a thriving online business, here are some ideas on how to build your list, set it up properly, and go about your email marketing campaigns:

- **Interact online**. By getting to know people personally, you can earn their trust and, eventually, ask them for their email. You can also ask friends and family for theirs.
- **Simply gather emails**. Even if you don't have a platform yet, they will come in handy.
- If you already have a website, **offer a free incentive**, like a short eBook or report. Make sure to have an opt-in form where the prospect can fill in their name and email – that's just the lead you need for your email list.
- When your website or landing/product page is all set, use an **email marketing tool** to build your campaigns. I recommend software such as MailChimp, AWeber, Drip, Constant Contact and ConvertKit.
- **Create an automated email sequence** for those very first leads that join your list. One should be a welcome email (it can include a discount or freebie), and a couple more can slowly introduce them to your products/services.
- Make sure each email is **useful or exciting.** Not every email should – obviously – be about sales. Directing subscribers to a new post on your blog is a great way to provide free information, tips and even entertainment.

- **Promote offers, giveaways and discounts** via email every so often. You can include coupon codes, particularly during festive seasons, international days, and for your subscriber's birthday.

Being online as much as possible and interacting with people is probably your most affordable option for now. And the best way to do it is via social media...

GROWING YOUR FOLLOWING WITH SOCIAL MEDIA

Social media marketing deserves its own book entirely. It's one the best way to generate traffic to your website and products. Why? Because over 3.6 billion people use social media and the number is projected to increase to 4.41 billion in 2025!

But how do you choose the best social media platform, aka network, for your business?

Here is a quick breakdown of the **features and audiences** per platform to help you make that decision:

- **Facebook** is used by nearly 3 billion users monthly. It's a great platform for startups and audiences over 30. It's also very community-geared thanks to the Groups option. But it's Business Pages that should be your focus here, as all digitally-minded businesses have such pages, no matter what their industry.

- **YouTube** is the second largest search engine after Google (and also *owned* by Google, who likes to promote it in search results). If you can pull off high-quality videos that relate to your products or services, YouTube is a superb option. It also caters to almost all age groups.
- **Instagram** is a visual platform. Promoting pictures or videos of your products might work well here, as long as your target audience is predominantly women aged between 18 – 34. All your images and videos must be high-quality, too, and make use of popular and niche-specific hashtags. Posting quite often to keep your follower engaged is also a necessity.
- **Twitter** is a platform for those who like to share their opinions on current events, news and debates. It's also the top announcement platform (preferred by politicians in particular). I recommend you use Twitter only to share news related to your products/services rather than voice your personal opinions, as the latter may hurt your brand.

- **LinkedIn** is geared towards B2B audiences. You can create a business page but it's highly unlikely that a customer will ever find your brand there. You may however end up meeting potential partners, collaborators and affiliates.
- **TikTok** is all the rage these days. The app boasts over 73 million users and is constantly growing! Some of the biggest brands are on the platform (Levi's, Zara, Ryanair, BMW, Marvel, Nando's, and more) so it may be worth playing around with the platform to see how it works for you. Communities are also a big thing on TikTok: BusinessTok and BrandTok are two niche communities where business leaders share tips and livestreams of their events.

Here are some ways to **grow your brand's following** through social media:

1. Start with one or two social media platforms – don't blast out on all of them. Just make sure your target audience frequents there.
2. Use tools like Canva to create interesting graphics and branded pictures to post on your social media. Random images that don't blend together won't make your brand interesting or memorable.

3. If you're recording videos, you can start by simply using your phone if it has an HD camera. Build up to more professional gear only when you can afford it. If you can't produce a good quality video, it's best to avoid video networks entirely.
4. Engage with those who comment on your images/videos. Be friendly and polite. You can use emojis to express feelings and add some personality to your comments.
5. Ask questions. This is another great way to engage with your audience. You can also create polls.

And there you have it – all the basic steps to setting up your online brand and growing it! But do keep in mind that, while learning the ropes of online business theoretically can be achieved by reading a book, you will have to actually apply the knowledge acquired before you can make any assessment or decision on whether or not it is the right kind of business for you.

And learning never really ends! Trends are constantly changing, society itself is changing (pandemics, anyone?), and technology is streamlining (and occasionally complicating) the world of online business. No one knows everything, because "everything" isn't fixed or set in stone. You have to be flexible, lenient, and ever eager to keep up with the constant changes and ensure your business is also keeping up with them.

And without further do, let's actually get started with some real, solid business ideas. The following chapters will unveil the most profitable online business models you can emulate to start a thriving Internet-based business...and work as passively as possible to get there.

Are you ready?

2

DROPSHIPPING

It is important to be vested in the knowledge of dropshipping if you are interested in online business. So many people do not fully comprehend this concept—but I'm going to comprehensively break it down for you.

The process of dropshipping can look intimidating at first. We'll cover what the term means, how you can make use of it to your advantage, and the things that guarantee success in this particular business model.

So, without further ado, let's move on to the business of the day!

WHAT IS DROPSHIPPING?

Let's begin with the definition of *dropshipping*:

> **Dropshipping** is an order fulfillment method wherein the business itself does not carry inventory, own a warehouse, manufacture, pack or ship orders. Instead, these tasks are performed by third-party partners.

As you can probably tell, dropshipping is a great system to adopt if you want to worry less about things. All you have to do is partner with a dropship supplier that manufactures or stores products, packages products, and ships them straight to your customer for you. Your only concerns would pertain mostly to management of the online business and making sure operations are running smoothly.

Still, not into it? Let's dive into this further for a better understanding of the process.

To simplify the whole thing, let's look at it from these angles:

1. **First**, a customer places an order for a product on your online store.
2. **Second**, you automatically or manually send the order and customer details to your dropship supplier.
3. **Lastly**, your dropship supplier prepares and ships the order directly to the information you forwarded beforehand - your customer.

This type of business is very enticing as it takes away the need for you to own a physical business location (an office, warehouse). All you need to own for this business is a functioning laptop and a strong internet connection at all times.

On the other hand, store owners that do own physical spaces can also use dropshipping for some goods. This enables them to do their business peacefully without worrying about ways to free up resources and space for their products.

Now let's look into some terminologies you should be aware of when getting into dropshipping business. Although these terms are usually used in the business world, they don't mean exactly the same thing when applied to dropshipping. They are:

Manufacturer

Under dropshipping, a manufacturer produces the products themselves. It is important to note that not all manufacturers have a dropshipping program. However, it is of great benefit for you if the manufacturer of the product you are interested in has one. If they do, it removes the trouble of inflated costs as a result of the middle man—vendor or supplier. When accumulated, these reduced costs can translate to a bigger profit margin.

Dropshipping Wholesaler/Supplier

A dropshipping wholesaler or supplier buys a product from its manufacturer in large quantity. They then move on to package and ship it to the online buyers through your e-commerce business.

Dropshipping Aggregator

A dropshipping aggregator is a person that buys varying products from different manufacturers. They do this to provide the retailer with a diversity of products to sell. With the aggregator in place, you don't have to worry about some of the cons of dropshipping. You don't have to worry about multiple wholesaler costs, spending a lot of time sending out different orders to multiple vendors. Also, you can now prevent mix-ups and delays in orders and shipments with this method.

However, you should know that these benefits do not come for free. Note that aggregators take a higher percentage of payments and this could affect your overall profit margins.

Now that you understand the terms, let's look into the reasons and benefits associated with dropshipping.

WHY DROPSHIPPING?

Dropshipping sounds like a great business model for a first-timer in the business world. It involves low-risk, low-investment, and doesn't seem so much like a gamble—unlike the conventional business model. The amount of capital required to go into establishing this business method is minimal. So, even people that own a store with an inventory can also try dropshipping to see the customers in the market before stocking up on it.

This business type is a fulfillment model used by many retailers around the world and is perfectly legal (make sure to emphasize that when your friends ask you!).

As with any other business, the key to having a successful dropshipping business remains the same: **Provide your customer with the best services and build a brand the attracts the right audience all the time.**

Most retail shops don't personally manufacture the product(s) they sell in their physical store. Dropshipping takes this approach and restructures it into a fulfillment model to fit an online business. Hard work is always required to kick-start this business model (like the traditional ones).

To gain a high profit margin, it is important to find the right area of specialization, as well as a reliable supplier. As a retailer, your profit margin will vary due to the type of goods you sell and the niche(s) you go for. Another good way to ensure higher margins is to source directly from the manufacturer. By doing this, you have phased out the middleman, thereby getting an increased profit, compared to dealing with a supplier.

BENEFITS OF DROPSHIPPING

There are many pros to the dropshipping business model. There are various aspects to these benefits—let's have a look at some of them:

- ✔ **No-fuss setup**

The setup of this business model is quite simple. You don't have to start searching for a large warehouse or workspace to begin trading. It just involves three simple steps that can be achieved from the comfort of your couch: **Find a reliable supplier, set up your website, and begin to sell goods to your customers.** This business type is quite easy to process, even for someone that has no background in the business world.

✔ **Low setup costs**

In conventional business models, the greater part of the cost is related to running the business operations, like purchasing inventory and space. Dropshipping cancels this. Now, the costs you have to take care of are those related to running your website—the hosting, software, apps etc.

✔ **Low overhead costs**

As a dropshipping business, you are not renting or buying an office space or warehouse, and not even purchasing stock. Paying for office electricity bills, phone bills, stationery, and so on are also out of the equation. The main cost you have to worry about is the stable cost of maintaining the website.

✔ **Considerably low business risk**

There is no pressure in having to sell your inventory before a due date, nor is overstocking applicable. Loss is rarely and aspect of this business model. Hence, if the business does not sell products, there is nothing to lose.

✔ **Location-independent**

The dropshipping business can be run from anywhere at any time since you don't need warehouses or employees. You can basically do business from the comfort of your home, the backseat of an Uber in motion, or on a beach in Hawaii. As mentioned earlier, the core necessities for this business type are your laptop and a strong internet connection.

✔ **Diversity of products to sell**

No matter what you are interested in selling, you can always find a dropship supplier for it. The choice is yours; you can specialize in one amazing product or spice things up by opting for a variety under one niche (think various smartphones brands as well as cases, batteries, and other accessories).

✔ **Abundance of time and resources to grow your business**

In the conventional business model, you have to put in much time, resources, and work effort to increase your profits. However, all you have to do with dropshipping is send more orders to your supplier and leave them to handle everything else. Doing this helps you earn more revenue and you are left with enough time to develop your business plans and capacity.

✔ **Losses are reduced on damaged products**

In dropshipping, the shipment is made directly from the supplier to the customer. Since there are fewer steps involved in this shipment process, it reduces the risks of delivering damaged goods due to an extended movement from one physical space to another.

SET UP YOUR SHOPIFY STORE WEBSITE

Shopify is a subscription-based commerce platform that integrates the buying and selling of tangible products. It manages payments, inventory and shipping, packing all processes neatly under one piece of software.

But don't be in a hurry to register with Shopify without having gone through all the necessary steps first:

1. Be intentional about beginning a dropshipping business

Mindset is the very first thing to establish here, no matter how cliché it may sound. As with other business models, it takes commitment, hard work, and a long-term view to make a new online business work. Do not approach your business with fairy tale expectations because, even though your business will be online, it is still a business in the *real* world. Be realistic about the investment needed and your profit potential so that you don't end up quitting.

> ➢ ***Expert tip:*** There are two major ways through which you can achieve a successful business. You don't have to dwell on both of them, you can just go ahead and pick one. They are **time** and **money**; which can you sacrifice?

2. Select an idea for your business

We spoke about niches in Chapter 1, and I will keep repeating it until it sinks in: Selecting a niche is one of *the most important steps* to building a profitable online business. Yes, you can be a Jack-Of-All-Trades, but you will be risking that profitability and your reputation. Start by investigating the **niche that really interests**

you and decide based on how you can make profits from it while *enjoying* the process.

> ➢ ***Expert tip:*** Not sure what sells best on the Shopify platform? Shopify can actually help you with that concern, as it lists trending products based on how frequently they are sold on the platform. Keep an eye on that list and you won't be sorry you did.

3. Research your competitors

Once you have chosen the product(s) you want to sell in your store, you should look into your **competitors** to understand their methods. If your market has a lot of competitors, then this is a good thing in dropshipping. Simply narrow your research down to a few dropshipping companies to help keep you focused to plan your winning strategy. Are they charging a certain price per product? Charge less. Are they offering seasonal discounts? Plan monthly discounts.

> ➢ ***Expert tip:*** Learn everything you can about every area of your competitors' businesses and keep an organized **spreadsheet** of them for easy reference. You can also conduct deeper research on your competitors via spy tools like SimilarWeb and Alexa.

4. Choose your supplier

There are two ways to find suppliers for your Shopify store:

- **Via a supplier database** like Dropship Direct, Alibaba, or AliExpress.
- Employ an **integrated supplier directory** in your store's backend, like Oberlo.

Oberlo is the easiest dropshipping process for Shopify stores. On the Oberlo marketplace, you can get millions of products through AliExpress and import them to your store with just a click of a button.

> ➢ ***Expert tip:*** Once you have a good and structural website, your job becomes so much easier. All you need to do is double-check if the order details are correct, then click the order button. The product then ships from the AliExpress dropshipping supplier to the customer, wherever they are.

5. Register and build your Shopify store

And you're here! Time to set up your actual store. Creating a Shopify store is a fairly straightforward process and can be broken down as follows:

Step #1: Create your account at www.shopify.com. You can start with a free trial.

Step #2: Add your products but don't rush. They each have to be accurately named and priced.

Step #3: Add your site pages. These usually include the Homepage, About, Privacy Policy, Terms of Service, Return Policy, Reviews, FAQ, Blog, and Contact. If you have trouble mastering words, hire a copywriter to assist you with the pages.

Step #4: Choose your Shopify template. Don't expect a barrage of complicated templates, as Shopify templates are simple and straightforward. Pick one that appeals to you and use the Shopify builder to tweak it accordingly. Some popular free templates to choose from are Supply, Brooklyn and Narrative.

Step #5: Set up your shipping. Go to the "Shipping" section in your Settings tab and select your preferred shipping locations, rates and carriers.

Step #6: Set up your tax details. You must also input your tax information here (consult your tax advisor first) so that Shopify can automatically calculate taxes per purchase.

Step #7: Set up your payments. Choose a payment gateway like Shopify Payments (but be aware that this supports transactions with only a number of countries) or a third-part payment processor.

Step #8: Launch your store! To launch your store to the world, you will have to select a Shopify plan. Basic Shopify, which is the most affordable plan, is currently priced at $29 – I recommend you opt for it as a brand-new store, then scale as the profits grow.

MARKET YOUR STORE AND PRODUCTS

Launching a new store is one thing. But how will potential customers know it exists? This is where marketing comes in.

Here are **10 strategies** you can use to market your new Shopify store:

1. Make use of **visual social media** such as Facebook, Instagram, Pinterest, YouTube, and TikTok. It's all about getting those products you sell seen!
2. Introduce a **referral program** to spread the existence of your business.
3. Get involved in joint **brand contests**.
4. **Give away coupons** and coupon codes. Do this from time to time.

5. **Blog.** Providing free and useful content your audience can learn from is greatly appreciated by them and makes your business come across as serious, current and active.
6. Use **email marketing**. Send out email campaigns announcing limited-time discounts, giveaways, coupon codes, new blog posts, and much more.
7. Utilize **Search Engine Optimization (SEO)**. This can be done by tweaking elements inside and outside your website via keywords. The goal is to get your website **ranked** higher in the search engine results, but you may need a pro to help you get there.
8. **Reward** customers for promoting you or reviewing your products.
9. Delve in **offline marketing**. Print a bunch of **flyers** and distribute them.
10. **Spread the word** among friends and family about your business to get loving criticisms and support.

AUTOMATING YOUR BUSINESS FOR PASSIVE INCOME

Time is a precious commodity that should not be underestimated when running a dropshipping business.

In the beginning, you have to do everything by yourself from marketing and management, to accounting and customer service, to mention but a few. At this stage, the success of your business depends entirely on you. However, you are human and you can't do all in 24 hours a day.

So what can you do to save time while also upping your earnings? **Automate the business**, of course!

> **Business automation** is the act by which you use technology to perform tasks that you would usually do manually when running your business.

Dropship automation is not so difficult as it can be achieved by using apps and software that are programmed to perform specific tasks. Note that many of these apps and software can be acquired for free.

Although it is not advisable to *completely* automate your dropshipping business, you should automate parts of it. This will help get you free space, avoid burnout, make more money, and grow faster.

There is a slew of **benefits** to automating your drop-shipping business:

✔ **It saves time**. Since automation works faster than you can, it can continue the good work while you take a break to eat, sleep, or watch movies. The bottom line is that it gives you spare time to focus on other parts of your life or business.

✔ **You save money**. Before the existence of automation, you would need to hire people to do the tasks you are too busy to perform. Automation lets you employ robots to do the time-consuming work you don't want to, for free or a small amount. However, this is just half of what you would have to pay for extra staff.

✔ **Accuracy**. Humans make mistakes…sometimes more than you can afford. Robots and systems on the other hand don't make as many. This prevents you from making a mistake on a customer's order, getting payments and refunds wrong, and so many other – often tedious – processes.

✔ **It prevents exhaustion**. Doing everything on your own might lead to you overworking yourself. Hence, this may result in a failing business when there's is too much for just one person to do. Automation delegates certain tasks to apps, preventing you from stress, worry, even a full-blown breakdown!

✔ **Work becomes passive.** You are not actively involved in selling your products, because the system is doing it for you. This is one of the most common methods employed to make a business a passive activity.

But what kind of automation can you put into effect? Some of the most popular **dropshipping automation tools** other than Shopify and Oberlo are:

- AliDropship
- Dropified
- Inventory Source
- Funnel Genie
- ClickFunnels
- Kartra
- Spocket
- ShopMaster
- Printify
- Modalyts
- Printful

There is so much potential when it comes to dropshipping. But there are more ways to sell tangible products online. I hope you are as excited about the next chapter as I am…

3

SELLING ON AMAZON

I've introduced you to the world of e-commerce and how to sell tangible products through the dropshipping model and Shopify. Now I want to introduce you to the "big boss": Amazon.

You may have already heard about **Fulfillment by Amazon,** also known as Amazon FBA. This program provides a unique way for online retailers to execute customer orders without bothering about handling, storage or logistics — Amazon takes care of all of that via its fulfillment center. In addition, Amazon supervises all storage and shipping needs and costs for your customers (for a fee). Does this ring a bell?

As with the dropshipping model, the only thing you have to do here is sell the products to your customers and take care of the marketing aspect of the business. Isn't this worth considering?

The FBA business model is different from the regular sales model on Amazon – don't deem them to be the same thing. Under the regular model, **sellers are in charge** of handling shipping, return costs and order fulfillment. All of these expenses can wear down the net profit a seller expects to gain.

FBA can be advantageous to certain retailers that wish to **eradicate excessive costs** in these unavoidable areas.

The steps below show an example of this arrangement:

1. A bag company sells bags on Amazon because of the unavailability of space to carry inventory for their customers. Amazon handles the inventory.
2. When someone purchases a bag, the order is conveyed to Amazon. Amazon then prepares, packages and ships the bag to the buyer.
3. The seller then presents a bit of the profit in fees to Amazon.
4. All the seller has to do is take care of the list of products and make sure that Amazon has enough products in storage to fulfill orders.

In summary, Amazon is responsible for most of the logistical work of online shopping.

Now, you may be wondering: **How much does Amazon FBA cost?** This depends entirely on the amount of product you want to use with this business type. The fees are typically based on the size and weight of the items stored on Amazon. On Amazon's product size level, lighter items are priced higher. Therefore, FBA might be too expensive to justify it for businesses that mainly sell low-dollar items.

In addition, Amazon's fulfillment fees increase as you store more inventory. Also, a higher item fee is charged if your stored items stay longer than 180 days in their storage. An online seller that doesn't rotate their items pays more money than a seller that does.

In essence, your FBA cost **can't be estimated** as there's no flat rate or prediction. Rather, Amazon provides a settlement fee report in your FBA dashboard to keep you updated. It is advisable to give the FBA a trial on a small scale to know your way around things. As time goes on, you'll be able to see how much the FBA service costs. Then, you can deduce results if you were to expand your inventory in the future.

Whether or not utilizing Amazon's FBA business model is beneficial to you depends on your budget and distinct needs. Therefore, it is important to check Amazon's FBA guidelines and regulations before using their service.

BENEFITS OF USING AMAZON FBA

Amazon FBA can be very beneficial. Let's dive into some interesting parts of Amazon FBA that make it attractive to online retailers.

- ✔ It is appropriate for people who sell **enormous** items that would be expensive to store typically. Such items include; furniture, workout equipment, TVs, to mention but a few.
- ✔ It makes it easy to run an online business with **less hassle.** Since Amazon takes care of all the logistics work on your behalf, this provides you time. Now, you can focus your energy and time on other parts of your online business.
- ✔ Amazon possesses **unlimited storage** space all over the world. Thus, you won't have to spend so much on shipping costs through FBA. Since there will be an Amazon store in your customer's location, this drastically reduces costs.
- ✔ With Amazon FBA, you **don't have to worry** too much about anything! Amazon handles

almost every aspect including customer service. What's there to worry about?

✔ Doing business via this medium makes your business more popular. This is because anything you sell via FBA automatically earns the Amazon **Prime** badge. This makes your customers qualified for Prime free shipping and quickened times.

GET STARTED WITH ONLINE ARBITRAGE

Amazon FBA is a form of *online arbitrage*:

Online arbitrage is the act of purchasing items at a lower cost from online streams and selling them back online at a higher price.

Online arbitrage is a legal venture that anyone can commit to. Online stores like Amazon have formal measures in place for the condition of items that you can sell. Also, they prevent the sale of fake products.

But there are also various **types of online arbitrage**. Let's look at all the methods that include Amazon:

- **Amazon Online Arbitrage**: This is the most famous platform to perform online retail arbitrage. It hosts more than two million sellers and draws in hundreds of millions of buyers monthly from all over the world.
- **eBay-to-Amazon Arbitrage:** This is not significantly different from other sourcing methods online. You discover a product on eBay at a reduced price and list it on Amazon for profit. However, know that many products on eBay are **used** ones. Therefore, you have to source carefully for **new** ones to be able to sell on Amazon.
- **Amazon to eBay Arbitrage:** In Amazon to eBay arbitrage, you **don't need to buy** goods from online retailers. You can just sell the items directly without purchasing them. Find an item on Amazon, then list it on eBay for a higher price. When you sell it, order it from Amazon and send it to the eBay buyer. It is as simple as that.

But there is a slew of other stores where you can **source resalable products** at, like:

- Walmart
- Home Depot

- Kohls
- Target
- JC Penney
- Lowes
- Sears
- Frys
- Best Buy
- Walgreens
- CVS
- Disney Store
- Shopko
- Vitacost
- Herbergers
- Bloomingdales
- Gamestop

Want to make your life a little easier when it comes to sourcing products you can resell? **Online arbitrage tools and software** can help you spot hidden deals and niches that are profitable via comparisons. They provide an advantage in listing and selling your products before your competitors have the chance. Some tools can communicate pricing and positioning history to help you to know the items trending, as well as keeping tabs on stable prices. They also provide you with a vivid comprehension of your expenses history and ways to manage them for profit's sake.

However, you have to be patient because it takes time to learn how to effectively use these tools. It is wise to opt for sourcing tools that can scan as many stores as possible. For instance, there are **repricing tools** that can help you reprice your items competitively. Examples of repricing tools are: Sellery, BQool, Repricing Central, Boostmyshop, and myPricing.

Free Online Arbitrage Tools

- Invisible Hand
- PriceBlink
- CamelCamelCamel
- Honey

Paid Tools and Software

- JungleScout
- Keepa
- Tactical Arbitrage
- Source Mogul
- ASINspector

Once you learn how online arbitrage operates, there is plenty of room to grow in skills, software and strategy. For example, you can incorporate sourcing lists, which you purchase or build over time. The more you can streamline your online arbitrage business, the less you will have to worry about getting things done.

WHOLESALING ON AMAZON

So far, we have been looking at the retail business model. With Amazon FBA and online arbitrage, you purchase discounted or cheap retail products to resell as pricier retail products for a profit. But what about wholesale? Is there any profit to be had in that — particularly when it comes to a complete newbie in the online business world?

The answer is a resounding YES! And you don't even have to leave the Amazon marketplace.

Amazon's sales platform caters to multiple sellers and buyers from all over the world. 26% of the sellers sell wholesale.

> **Wholesale** is a method of buying bulk branded products from another manufacturer, supplier, or distributor to resell to consumers.

As you can probably tell, there are some differences between the wholesale model and other models we've spoken about previously. Let's take a closer look at the differences between wholesale and the other business models you are already aware of:

Wholesale vs Arbitrage	Wholesale vs Dropshipping
Arbitrage is the process of buying products from retail stores at a discounted price to resell on Amazon. Similar to wholesalers, resellers buy branded products they can sell. Contrary to the arbitrage process, wholesalers buy in bulk rather than individually.	**Dropshippers** list goods to sell on Amazon. Once a purchase is confirmed, they place an order via the supplier or manufacturer of the product who ships the product on behalf of the dropshipper.
Wholesalers arrange rates with suppliers and manufacturers directly. On the other hand, resellers purchase discount products via retail to sell through retail.	**Wholesalers** on the other hand own their inventories and are in control of shipping orders by themselves.

There are also many **benefits** to be had if you opt to go with Amazon wholesaling:

- ✔ **Product demand**. You can sell big brands (Apple, Samsung, etc) that buyers are actively searching for. This takes the marketing pressure off your business.
- ✔ **Quick to get started**. After retail arbitrage, wholesale is the simplest business model to get up and running. According to Jungle Scout's study of thousands of Amazon sellers, about 51% of wholesalers spent less than six weeks to set up their business.
- ✔ **Profitable**. According to recent statistics, you

can begin to acquire significant profit margins in under three months.

✔ **Scalable and passive**. No need to focus on building a brand or creating listings. Instead, you can concentrate on your growth and even build a team to manage your daily operations.

Selling wholesale on Amazon is an effective business opportunity. However, there are a lot of things you need to be aware of before properly going into it. Here are the **fundamental steps** to follow before you can successfully sell wholesale on Amazon:

1. Set up a seller account.
2. Discover a high-demand product or line of products to sell.
3. Contact the manufacturer to make an inquiry about the particular product.
4. Build an optimized listing to rank against your competitors.
5. Introduce and promote the product you settle on.
6. Organize and develop your business—inventory, sales, and so on.

As a wholesale seller, you will also need to get a **wholesale license**. This might be called different names in different regions, ranging from a business license to a tax-exempt form, depending on the country you reside in. Ensure that you check out the wholesale license requirements as they are stated in your country or state.

Ways to ship wholesale orders through Amazon

There are two options available to fulfill your Amazon sales. They are through the Fulfillment by Amazon (FBA) and Fulfillment by Merchant (FBM).

As we have seen, **Fulfillment by Amazon** is a program which offers you to ship your products to Amazon's fulfillment centers for storage. After you sell your products, Amazon picks, packs, and ships the products on your behalf. This takes a lot of pressure off your new business and leaves you with no stress when shipping your goods. Also, the FBA cost for shipping your products is often less than when you ship them yourself. If you are selling products that turn over slowly or are oversized, FBA may not be the best option for your business.

Fulfillment by Merchant, on the other hand, may be the optimal fulfillment procedure for your business. Contrary to FBA, FBM sellers don't have to pay Amazon a fee for taking care of their orders because they are responsible for picking, storage, packaging, and shipping themselves.

Wholesale is another lucrative way to make income from selling on Amazon. But there is one more rather profitable Amazon selling method I want to share with you…

AMAZON PRIVATE LABEL EXPLAINED

Selling and reselling another brand's product is one thing. But what if the brand was your own?

I'm not talking about becoming Apple or Samsung (I'm pretty sure none of us can actually afford that). I'm talking about creating your own private label for the products you sell. Let's me explain.

Amazon Private Label is an opportunity to enhance your Amazon revenue through branding. It is essentially an advanced version of *Amazon FBA*.

Amazon Private Label is the process of finding generic products that are already in demand on Amazon and developing your unique package and signature for them.

But why should you consider this particular Amazon business model? Here are some reasons and benefits to wrap your mind around:

- ✔ **There's a massive market** for private label products on Amazon to tap into. According to the Private Label Marketing Association (PLMA), private label sales totaled $158.8 billion in 2020 (an 11.6% increase from 2019).
- ✔ **Lower competition**, as there is no need to compete for your unique brand name.
- ✔ **No restrictions** from the **brand owner.**
- ✔ You're in charge of the product's **style, design and packaging.**
- ✔ You can **maintain lower prices** while controlling profit margins, beating the competition, and attracting more customers.
- ✔ You can access **more suppliers**.
- ✔ You **don't need to create another store** or use another platform.
- ✔ You can constantly **tweak and improve** your product listings.

Does that tickle your fancy at all? I'm sure you want to dive right into the process and set up your account. But don't rush — there are different steps to take to ensure that you **develop your own Amazon Private Label business** successfully:

Step #1: Brainstorm product options. You can do your research on Amazon, Kickstarter, and so on for inspiration about what to sell. You can make it something you can sell all year round and make sure it is not restricted, or a product that needs Amazon's approval.

Step #2: Perform market research to make sure that the item you are interested in is worth selling.

Step #3: Check out potential suppliers for the product you chose. Alibaba is a good platform to look for suppliers because they allow you to buy items in bulk from manufacturers from different countries.

Step #4: Design your logo and packaging. This is what makes your product yours; you can even put the logo on the product if you wish. In all, provide nice packaging that will boost your customers' experience and include your website URL within the packaging.

Step #5: Decide how you will fulfill the orders. An easy way is to use Fulfillment by Amazon (FBA). That is, you can just send your products to Amazon and they will help you pack and ship the products, and also handle customer service.

Step #6: Develop your Amazon listing. Ensure that the picture you post is of high quality and come up with a title that will be noticed when potential buyers search for the item. Also, use bullets to list the features when describing your product.

Step #7: You can **boost your product's sales by optimizing its listing**. You can use Amazon PPC, and their in-house advertising system to place you top in the search results. You can also tweak your keywords to make them attractive.

Setting up an Amazon Private Label is a fairly straightforward process but it does require that you follow each step diligently. Because branding and packaging are integral parts of the process, it may be wise to consult a creative agency or graphic designer initially. If you're a bit of a creative yourself, the process will be much easier and much more enjoyable.

And now, our Amazon selling journey will have to come to its end...though it may surprise again fairly soon.

4

AFFILIATE MARKETING

We've looked into dropshipping, selling retail, selling wholesale, even creating your own private label to boost revenue. But what if you could eliminate most if not all those processes and still makes sales?

To do this, you can become an affiliate.

WHAT IS AFFILIATE MARKETING?

Let's start, as always, with a simple definition of *Affiliate Marketing*:

Affiliate Marketing is the process of promoting other people's products in exchange for a small commission for each sale made.

This concept of affiliate marketing is not a new or foreign idea — you have probably seen it around or have clicked on an affiliate link yourself. And it is such a popular form of marketing, that **40% of marketing professionals** quote affiliate marketing as the most desired digital skill.

Just like every other business model, affiliate marketing also is constituted of different elements that make it a successful and effective system. Let's take an in-depth look into how this whole thing works and what each role entails:

The Merchant

The merchant is known by a lot of names such as *the creator, the seller, the brand, the vendor,* or *the retailer.* This individual creates the product and it can be a big company or a single party. Hence, ranging from a single entrepreneur to startups to huge Fortune 500 companies, just anyone could be the merchant in charge of an affiliate marketing program. With these people, it does not matter if they are personally involved or not. All they need to have is a product to sell.

The Affiliate Marketers

The individual that falls in this category is also referred to as *the publisher.* Affiliates range from solo individuals to an entire company, so this job can result in earning a few hundred dollars in commissions every month or tens of millions of dollars. Marketing begins with these individuals. As an affiliate, one gets to promote one or numerous affiliate products. Also, this puts the affiliate marketers in charge of attracting and convincing potential buyers of the value the merchant's product has so that they end up buying it.

The Consumer

The *consumer, customer,* or *buyer* makes the affiliate system circulate. If there are no sales, there will be no commission or revenue to distribute. Therefore, the affiliate will try to market to the consumer via whatever medium they like. It might be through a social network, search engine using content marketing on a blog, digital billboards, and so on.

The Affiliate Network

The *affiliate network* is considered as part of the affiliate marketing equation. Most times, a network serves as the middleman between the affiliate and the merchant. Even though you promote someone's products and arrange a direct revenue share with them, it is still not enough. If you let a network like ClickBank or ShareASale take care of the payment and product delivery, it puts your affiliate marketing in a good light.

In some cases, affiliates may have to promote the product via an affiliate network. This happens in cases where the merchant manages their affiliate program on that particular network. Also, the affiliate network serves as a database of lots of products from which the affiliate marketer can pick which to promote.

Now that we got the terms out of the way, let's look into some of the actual **benefits of Affiliate Marketing:**

- ✔ Less cost of startup
- ✔ Minimum ongoing costs
- ✔ Minimum risk
- ✔ Targeted Traffic
- ✔ Flexibility
- ✔ Maximum ROI

Here are some **further reasons** you should consider Affiliate Marketing as your next online business venture:

✔ **You can work with what you want.**

In this line of work, you are the boss of yourself. This means that you are in charge of deciding what your Affiliate Marketing website should be all about. You can select whatever niche you prefer as well as the topics to give information on.

✔ **You can work whenever you please or completely passively.**

There is no fixed timeframe to when you can and cannot carry out Affiliate Marketing. You may decide to spend 15 hours working one day, spend 10 hours the next day, or even take the day off. If a functional affiliate link is sitting on your website or embedded in your ads, then the work is being done for you without your active presence required (passive income).

✔ **You don't have to source or directly sell any product.**

With Affiliate Marketing, you don't need to sell any product or service, find suppliers, source manufacturers, negotiate rates and all that. All that is in the description of this job is recommending products to various people that may benefit from them or find certain value in them. Hence, you are not directly selling anything.

✔ There is no need to have an inventory of products.

As an Affiliate Marketer, you don't need to own any products. You just have to recommend products and get your commission if someone happens to buy. For instance, let's say you recommend a beautiful and classic bag from Amazon that is a great choice for women in your blog post. Leslie enjoyed reading the blog post and clicks through to Amazon to buy the bag. Through this process, you have just made a commission on the fashion bag without even purchasing or owning the item.

✔ You aren't involved in tedious processes, like handling returns or complaints.

As an Affiliate Marketer, you get to be involved in the fun part of the whole process. However, you are not concerned when there are returns or complaints about the products. This means that you are not contacted if there is any defect in the product purchased. Rather, the buyer contacts Amazon (or other business websites) or the seller directly to fix the issue. You don't have to deal with complaints because you just recommended the product and didn't sell it.

✔ **You can earn money all-day long.**

Since there is no time frame to working as an affiliate marketer, you can earn money with your recommendations 24/7. You can even make money while asleep as you don't have to be present on the site for someone to purchase the product you recommend. The commission from the product purchased is transferred automatically to your affiliate account for you to cash out later. This is an easy and hassle-free method to earn money, isn't it?

✔ **There is low cost and maintenance.**

To begin your own Affiliate Marketing business, the first thing you will need to kick-start the business is a website. To own a website is cost-friendly compared to starting a franchise or brick and even mortar business. The only fee you have to pay is the hosting and domain fee. They are both affordable compared to other businesses.

✔ You acquire more free time to focus on other areas of life.

Being an affiliate marketer gives you the time to concentrate on other important areas of life. For instance, as a mom, you get to spend more time with your family. Also, can have your workspace at home which makes you available to your kids all the time. Since you can take your work with you everywhere, there are no restrictions to things you can and can't do.

GET STARTED WITH AFFILIATE MARKETING

The process of being an affiliate marketer is not so difficult. They are simple steps that can be easily achieved if you are up for working as an affiliate marketer.

To start with, you will need to **discover an affiliate program or network** that interests you. Then, you can begin to create content with the inclusion of the custom links the program provides. These links track your progress as you will be given a commission every time buyers purchase a product via them.

In addition, you can make up your mind to work with individual companies or affiliate networks where you can sign up and select the programs you are interested in. The selection process won't take long as it has been made easier by being divided into categories. The moment you become accepted, you can begin to promote your affiliate links. You can promote them via different mediums like social media, newsletters, on your website, and other places online that permit you to share links.

The moment you reach the minimum payment level, the network sends you your money. However, note that the payment method varies. It can be made via bank transfers, checks, and PayPal.

Let's break down the steps into a more concise formula:

Step #1: Select the product you want to promote.

Step #2: Search for the affiliate program available for the product you selected. View the overview of the program; this entails the type of products or services they render, payment procedure, and the commissions they offer. If you are content with this setup, you can apply and wait for confirmation that you have been accepted.

> ➢ **Expert tip:** There are various Affiliate Marketing Networks to choose from. I recommend looking at:

- **ClickBank:** One of the forefathers of affiliate marketing networks, ClickBank boasts over 200 million dollars in annual sales made by the 6 million entrepreneurs registered on the platform. It houses 276 categories and 21562 product listings, with 200 million customers spread across 190 countries. The platform is easy to use, features a large selection of products, and offers high commission rates – up to 75% and more!
- **ShareASale:** Home to more than 4,500 affiliate programs for merchants, this platform is perfect for both physical and digital products. On the digital side, you will discover lots of hosting providers, WordPress themes, and plugin shops. More than 1,000 merchants that work with this network do not work elsewhere. So, if you choose to work here, you will have access to exclusive merchants.
- **Awin:** This marketing platform gives you access to more than 13,000 different merchants. Although Awin acquired ShareASale in 2017, the two still run as two separate platforms and fish in different waters. Some of the big fishes they work with include HP, Etsy, Gymshark, StubHub, AliExpress, to mention but a few.

Awin also offer a low minimum payout - only $20

- **CJ Affiliate:** Formerly known as Commission Junction, you will find thousands of merchants under this roof. Here, you will be able to connect with about 2,696 different big and small merchants. Some of the big physical and digital companies you will find here are Grammarly, GoPro, Lowes, Office Depot, and Priceline. You can personally apply to these merchants from the dashboard.
- **Rakuten Marketing:** Formerly known as LinkShare, this famous network houses famous merchants such as Walmart, Best Buy, Macy's and Papa Johns. You can also find smaller merchants here to select from. Rakuten also comes with some nice features to enhance productivity.
- **Avangate Affiliate Network:** This network is concentrated on digital goods and software instead of physical products. You get access to popular software merchants like Bitdefender, Kaspersky, Awario, and more than 22,000 pieces of software. You can also get paid through PayPal receive and high commissions (over 50%).

Step #3: Register for the affiliate program. Once you've signed up, you get a special link that gives access to the merchant to be able to trace the people who clicked your link.

Step #4: Start promoting the product. Once you have acquired your affiliate link, you can just go on it promote it whether on Amazon or any other website. When they buy a product using your special link, you will automatically get a commission for the purchase.

> ➢ **Expert tip:** There are different mediums through which you can promote the link. You just have to think about which of the ways will be easy and very much convenient for you. **A blog** is one of the ways through which you can start your affiliate marketing. What's key here to develop content in different forms to boost the product you are marketing for. Your content may be in form of tutorials, review posts, resource pages, or even emails. Use whatever medium to pass across your recommendation message, as long as you do not forget to add your link.

Step #5: Use Google Analytics to gauge sales and also track your rankings via Google. If your affiliate sales aren't making much of a commission, maybe you should come up with another product idea at this point. If you are seeing great results, just keep going!

Step #7: Successfully complete this process and repeat.

The steps are all easy to implement. As soon as you find an affiliate network that works for you, you can start scaling your venture with more and more products and affiliate links.

AMAZON ASSOCIATES

Now, I would like to introduce you to a specific Affiliate Marketing Network, known as **Amazon Associates**.

Amazon Associates is similar to other affiliate networks — except that Amazon is the biggest online marketplace worldwide. You're dealing with a real giant here.

The process to register with Amazon Associates is simple: once you've registered for the Amazon Associates program, all you need to do is to provide recommendations for Amazon products and provide links to buy them through your published content. Once a reader clicks your link and purchases the product, Amazon pays you a commission. This is not only for that linked product, but also for all eligible products your reader buys from Amazon within the next 24 hours.

It is important to note that you can only get paid when a reader actually makes a purchase. So, if they only click on the link to visit Amazon, you won't earn anything.

The Amazon Associates program is available for websites, blogs, social network channels, YouTube, and even mobile apps.

There are a few **things to be aware of** before you apply for the Amazon Associates program:

- To promote products, **you still need a website or blog** with solid content and an audience, just as you would if you promoted any affiliate product.
- Regardless of the platform you use, you must ensure that the content is of **high quality** so that it gives value to your readers and hopefully to you too.
- You should also have published at least **10 blog posts or articles** on your website. Also, most of them should have been updated within the last month.
- You have to also establish your website or blog

and **gain some decent traffic**. Although there is no traffic required to apply initially, you will need constant traffic to remain in the program.

Why is all the above so important? I'll tell you why: Once you have had **three qualified sales** within the first 180 days of your joining, **Amazon will review the sites** you gave during the application process. However, if Amazon deems the site given to be of low-quality, the application will be rejected. See now why your platform and its content are so important? According to Amazon, only high-quality sites can give their buyers a good experience.

Note that once your application is rejected, you will lose all that you have earned to that moment.

There are some **further limitations** when it comes to using the program:

- **You can't buy things for yourself.** This is because Amazon deducts anything you buy for personal use through your links. Also, they do the same for people they determine to have a relationship with you.
- Your site should not be a part of the sites **listed as unsuitable**. If your site is a part of the

"Unsuitable Sites", then you cannot apply for the program at all.

- You can't use **private groups or membership sites** as your registered website. It must be a platform that is accessible to all.

But what makes Amazon Associates so popular despite these minor limitations for affiliates?

Amazon Associates is popular because of its **large product catalog** that provides a wide range of opportunities to make money online. In almost every market, you can find their physical goods for sale. Also, there are tons of categories with millions of products to promote to your audience.

Furthermore, Amazon is very **good at selling products**. There's little wonder why they capture about 49% of all e-commerce traffic. They have been around a long time, selling products online for more than 21 years. Thus, they have enough experience in promoting products and converting customers all over the world.

Amazon is additionally popular because of the **good customer service** people have enjoyed over the years. Similarly, Amazon Associates is quite famous because of the success people have had over the years whilst using the Amazon affiliate program.

Let's now compare the pros and cons of using the Amazon Associates program side by side:

Pros	Cons
Amazon's large-scale size. Amazon is a high-traffic and trusted website where people come to do their businesses. They have over 90 million Prime members. These members are more likely to purchase from Amazon than other stores because of the shipping time frame among other benefits. In summary, they have a large internet presence that gives you opportunities and a large number of products.	**Your website should be on par with what Amazon likes.** You need a website that will appeal to Amazon, convince them of good high-quality content, be active, and have at least some decent traffic. Otherwise, there is no point in registering, not for Amazon, nor for you.
Great selling experience. Amazon is well-vested in how to convert customers and get them to purchase items. They also make use of the latest artificial intelligence technology to work their website and create the recommended products categories. As an Amazon affiliate, you will have the tools to help you sell on mobile.	**Low affiliate commission.** Amazon's affiliate commission rates range from 4% to 10%. Compared with other affiliate networks, Amazon pays the modest rate (which is, essentially, the lowest in most cases).
Diverse opportunities. You earn commission on everything your visitors purchase in the 24 hours after they click the affiliate link. This includes items that you didn't give a product link to. Also, the Amazon conversion upselling machine works continuously. This means that even if your reader clicks on the link to buy just one item, Amazon will work hard to get the additional items.	**Limited timeframe to sell.** Cookies last for only 24 hours. If your website visitor has clicked on your affiliate link but has failed to make a purchase from Amazon within 24 hours, you will not receive a commission. Unfortunately, many buyers do take their time before deciding to make a purchase.
No fees. You don't need to pay any fee to join the Amazon Associates Program.	**You can't use PayPal.** PayPal figuratively dominates the payment system, but Amazon does not support or integrate with this popular payment method. This applies to both buyers and sellers — as an affiliate, you too cannot expect to be paid via PayPal.

Accessibility. The Amazon Associates Program is accessible to anyone with a website or blog.	**Strict rules.** All of Amazon's rules and regulations must be followed strictly and at all times. If not, you may face banishment from the program.
Great customer service. Amazon boasts the best customer service and relevant experts. You won't have to worry about customer dissatisfaction when you recommend a solid product.	**No control over product quality.** If someone buys an Amazon-listed product that you recommended and it turns out to be faulty or dissatisfying in any way, that person may never trust your recommendations again. This is why you should ideally test out the product yourself before recommending it.
Tools. Their reporting tools help you sell more. They provide a reporting dashboard to give you the feedback needed to optimize your promotions.	**Email marketing is not permitted.** You can't use an Amazon affiliate link directly in your emails.
Preferred payment options. You have the option of being paid directly via a direct deposit into your bank account or Amazon gift cards. Checks are an option but there is a 15% processing fee - unless you are outside the U.S. in which case the fee is waived.	**Income is unpredictable.** Income via Amazon Associates is unpredictable. Commission rates and programs are not set in stone. They are so flexible that they may not always be in your favor.

Thankfully, some of the pros really do outweigh the cons, but you should still make considerations and weigh them against your own capabilities, skillset, time and investment.

If you're still pumped about becoming an Amazon Associates affiliate, here are the exact steps to follow to **register and set up your first account**:

Step #1: Go to Amazon Associates and choose the join now for free at the top-right corner. A sign-in page will help you to log into your existing account or create a new one.

Step #2: You will be shown the Account Information screen. This will auto-update your name, address, and phone number from your Amazon account. Just confirm the information provided.

Step #3: The Website and Mobile App List screen will appear. Add your website address here.

Step #4: Complete your profile, traffic, and monetization methods. Here, the preferred Associates' Store ID is your username (usually your website address).

Step #5: Move on to the Identity Verification screen and fill in the required fields.

Viola! You've just created your Amazon Associate account.

7 WAYS TO MARKET AFFILIATE PRODUCTS

Now that you have your website and have registered for Amazon Associates, it is not difficult to perform your duties as an affiliate marketer — that's right; this is what you should start calling yourself!

As a brand-new affiliate marketer, you will probably be wondering about the best ways to market your affiliate products. Below are some techniques you can begin to employ asap:

1. Social media campaigns. This is one of the simplest methods to promote and market your affiliate products.

> ➢ **Expert tip:** One of the most common ways to do this is by uploading a video on YouTube reviewing a product you love and then popping the Amazon affiliate link in the description for anyone who may want to purchase it.

2. Search Engine Optimization. SEO is a process that increases the visibility of your website through organic searches. It's all based on researching keywords that people search for the most and applying them to your platform. If you plan to use affiliate links to sell coffee machines, for instance, you should look up keywords that relate to this product (i.e. Nespresso coffee machine, espresso coffee machine, filter coffee machine, etc) and place them on your website, in your articles, social media, and so on.

> ➢ **Expert tip:** An SEO expert may be able to assist you if you have no idea how to go about keyword research and positioning.

3. Blogging. This is one of the fundamental processes of product promotion. You can write about any products you like and include your link anywhere within the body as anchor (hyperlinked) text. Your blog articles can be about any kind of topic that relates to your affiliate product (i.e. a piece on "Tips for New Hikers" where you can add links to hiking gear they can purchase), or it can be a review about the product itself (or even a list of products, like "The Top 10 Hiking Gear Items That May Save Your Life").

> ➢ **Expert tip:** Make use of your keywords in your blogs, too.

4. Emails or newsletters. While you cannot add Amazon affiliate links directly into an email, you can send an email to direct subscribers to your website where they can then peruse your content and click on any affiliate links embedded within in. That way you don't just send people to Amazon, but to your own website as well — and that's great for boosting traffic and hits.

> ➢ **Expert tip:** You can also link images in your emails. For example, you can add a picture of yourself wearing a watch or lipstick you have an affiliate link for (just make sure to use a link that

directs to your website, not the actual product). Your image can also have wording on it, like "Click here to read the article".

5. Include banners and buttons on your website. Adding a banner advertisement and call-to-action buttons is a nice way to grab your readers' attention and compel them to take action. This helps them click on important links — in this case, your affiliate links.

> ➢ **Expert tip:** Banners and buttons should be appealing to the eye and of high quality. Do not hesitate to hire a designer for the best results here.

There is so much that can be achieved through a website alone. And it's not just affiliate sales. Join me in the next chapter where will get into the real magic behind owning and operating a profitable website.

5

NICHE WEBSITES

We discussed affiliate marketing in the previous chapter and stressed the point of having a website prior to testing out this online business model. That website will need to have a **specific concentration** – or *niche* – and this is what we are going to discuss in this chapter.

So, what then is a *niche website*? This is something that is frequently mentioned among people in the online business.

A **niche website** is a website that concentrates on a specific interest, topic, or theme that is similar to a narrow group of people in a larger market.

A niche website focuses on an extremely particular term that people type into search engines. It provides its visitors with helpful and high-quality content to answer questions or solve problems popular among searchers.

This may all remind you of Chapter 1, where we got into niches and niching down your online business idea as a means of standing out among your competitors and accessing your target audience easier. A niche website is precisely created in that same vein.

The goal of a niche site is to provide its visitors with quality and helpful content that talks about anything they are searching for. Thus, it gives answers or solves problems that those visitors share among themselves. This, in short, is the purpose of a niche website.

WHY WOULD YOU NEED A NICHE WEBSITE?

There are numerous ways to make money online today that you can pick from. However, almost all of the points boil down to one basic thing: **owning a website**. If you don't have a website, then you can't get to play the online business game. It would be like going to the battlefield without the proper ammunition; you can't win the war. The same applies to the e-commerce world: you can't succeed in if you don't have a website.

The moment you start a niche website can be the first step to so much goodness coming your way. The skills you develop and learn from starting a niche business stick with you forever. Also, you can use the niche website-building process for almost any other business model you might want to get involved in down the line.

The aim of owning a niche website is to become the number #1 source of information on the internet for that specific niche. This is how you narrow down your potential audience and target them. **Target audiences** are an important part of developing your niche website.

This is because:

- They are useful for generating more income when on-site.
- It is easier to sell to this audience directly since they are already all interested in what you have to offer.
- Advertisers are very much interested in narrowing down their target. Therefore, you will be able to sell advertising at an extremely high price.
- You can promote products as an affiliate marketer that every one of your readers/audience will be interested in.
- You can release additional sites, services, or even software to your audience with ease through your niche website.

Here are some of the reasons you may want to set up a niche website:

✔ **It's a minimum investment.**

Stating any kind of brick-and-mortar business normally requires thousands of dollars' worth of investment, plus the overhead that comes with actually running the business. When it comes to a niche website on the other hand, you can build your site up for less than a few hundred dollars. You'll need a domain name which may cost as little as $10 per year, a hosting service which on a basic shared plan can cost as little as $3 a month, and possibly even a premium theme to get you up and running, but in total you shouldn't expect to pay more than $200 — and that's a one-time investment.

✔ You can write about topics that really interest you.

Your niche website can be about any topic you want it to be: sports, tech, home and garden, DIY crafts, nutrition, fitness, outdoors, you name it. All you have to do is find the industry you love to talk about the most and find relevant services or products to promote on it!

✔ You can gain work experience and earn expert status.

Instead of working for the "big man" and toiling away for 40 hours a week to gain work experience, you can set up a niche website. Why work for a tech retailer on a minimum wage when you can be selling tech gadgets yourself? You would certainly gain more insider knowledge into the industry and even become a real expert down the line. Stuck at a retailer job, you would simply be doing the same year in and year out – serving customers and striving to sell products while constantly being supervised and critiqued. If you start a niche website and do the work all by yourself, you're going to learn all the things that business managers are well aware of (more than your supervisor!) and how to run a proper business hands-on. By owning a niche website, you build your skill-set; something you can build from the scratch (nothing) to something you can be very proud of.

✔ **Passive income is easily attainable.**

A niche website is a perfect way to enter the world of passive income. This does not mean that it does not require real and hard work. It just means that once the work is done, then it is done. All that is left is for you to enjoy the rewards of your hard work and consistency via the money you make indefinitely. If the first sale happens while you are asleep, it will be an unforget-table experience.

You can further automate the business through tools and systems. You can also outsource the work you would rather not do, like customer support, email handling, or website maintenance.

✔ **Versatility of monetization options.**

There are so many ways to make money from your niche website. Be it via monetizing your content (like a blog), using display ads, or selling actual products (yours or others'), there is a wealth of opportunity to make versatile revenue via such a model. We will break down exactly how to monetize a niche website in the next sub-chapter.

I would now like to dispel some **myths around niche websites** before we actually dive into the actual site-building process:

Myth #1: ***You need to be an expert to have a niche website.***

On the contrary, you can earn expert status *by* setting up a niche website! But it is still a good idea to have some expertise on the topic you have selected, simply to reinforce your authenticity and instill further trust in your audience.

Myth #2: ***The more profitable the niche, the more money you can expect to make.***

A profitable niche may translate to a hungry crowd that constantly throws money at niche-related products, but it may also imply competition. Usually, the more profit is derived from a niche, the more competitive it will become. For instance, stocks, real estate, finance, and business are trending niches today — but nothing is stopping you from selecting one of these popular niches; it just means that you are going to have to put in extra legwork to get noticed.

Myth #3: ***Your website will always be one of the smaller fish in a huge pond.***

Starting small will undoubtedly be a daunting experience. You may not be able to become the next Livestrong or Buzzfeed, but you can still offer valuable content and leave your mark. In fact, why would you even want a huge website with an equally huge following? Think of all the content that would need to be put together on a daily basis, the multiple marketing and social media efforts, the teams and people that you would require for support of the business. That is a gigantic undertaking for someone just getting started in the business. An inexperienced marketer is going to be learning the ropes of the niche business for months if not years before they can attain that level of influence. I would still advise you work hard, be consistent, and be determined that you can, at some point, create and sustain a larger, more impactful niche website (honestly, don't give up!).

Myth #4: ***A niche website isn't worth the hassle if there's no profit to be had.***

Truly, a niche website that yields little to no revenue may feel like a lost cause. But don't make any definitive call once the site is still new. It may take months or even years to start seeing some good profit rolling in — just keep going until things pick up, as it will all be based on your effort to create great content and drive readers to your pages. There's also another aspect to consider: if you're creating a niche website merely for the purpose of profit, you might back out when things get tough. However, if you are in because you are truly interested in the topic you are dealing with, you will continue to enjoy what you are doing even if it does not yield as much profit as you expect it should.

Thus, your first niche ever should be about these two things; **something you are knowledgeable** about or **something you are interested in becoming knowledgeable** about.

SET UP AND MONETIZE YOUR NICHE WEBSITE

Developing a niche site can be an easy feat. All you need to do is make sure of three things, then you can successfully build yourself a niche site:

1. Set up a website with your domain and hosting.
2. Publish content targeting particular niche-specific keyboards.
3. Direct reliable, niche-audience traffic to your website (referral traffic, ads and SEO are the most popular techniques used to achieve this).

Now, it's time to select your niche but how do you go about that when it comes to actually building a website (not just coming up with a business idea as we spoke about in Chapter 1)? The following step-by-step process is the best way to get started:

Step #1: What do you know?

Start by listing at least ten things you know or are experienced in. Pen down these thoughts rather than just keeping them in your head. Also, you don't have to think too much about what to write. Just write what comes to your mind in about 5 to 10 minutes. The following are some questions that can keep you running with ideas on what to settle on:

- What do you know how to do best?
- What topic(s) do you know a lot about?
- When free, what research or reading do you get caught up in for fun?
- Do people ask for your take about anything? What is it?
- What do people always discuss when around you?
- What subjects were you extremely good at in school?
- Do you have any noteworthy accomplishments or achievements? What are they?
- What are you very much proud of?
- Don't overthink the process, just go with the flow.

Step #2: What piques your curiosity?

This step is similar to the first one. The only difference is that rather than jotting down what you know, you jot down what interests or arouses your curiosity. When you write about a topic, it forces you to understand the concept and become an expert at it. Here are some questions to keep the decision a bit easier:

- What TV shows do you watch?
- What was your career choice when you were younger?
- When you visit the bookstore, what section draws your attention?
- What magazine do you read?
- What do you never get enough if and want to know about more?
- If you could do anything and get paid for it full-time, what would you pick?
- What do you do for fun that you would like to improve on?
- What websites do you read?

As mentioned in the previous step, don't think too much about the answers to these questions. Just say what comes to your mind first without a doubt.

Step #3: Analyze your lists and select.

At this point, you have several lists of things to choose from. Now, all these questions can be narrowed down to one key question: What topic will you enjoy learning, reading, and writing about every day *without getting tired?*

Don't forget that it has to be something that interests you. It should also be capable of keeping you committed even at the sign of disengagement from readers. Try following these steps to pick the appropriate niche for you and you won't regret your choice.

Step #4: Check the competition.

As discussed in Chapter 1, you will need to look into your competitors to know who you will be coming up against. Make a list of the various websites that resemble the niche site you want to build. If your niche is smartwatches and tech gadgets, check out similar review sites, blogs, and social media channels to gauge their look, their style and their strategy, but most importantly look at their reviews and ratings; what are their followers saying? What are they raving about? And what solutions do the they need that the particular niche website isn't offering and you can?

Step #5: Build your website.

Pick a website builder like Wix, Squarespace or Weebly if you're feeling creative, or hire a web designer to set you up on Wordpress. Make sure to have your branding in place, connect your social media, and add important pages like a Blog or Reviews page.

Step #6: Get SEO sorted out.

Search Engine Optimization deserves its own book, but since I'm here to give you the very basics, I would advise you either learn all about SEO or hire an SEO expert to get you sorted here. The task would involve on and off-page SEO, optimizing each of your pages, images, meta descriptions, tags, along with your posts once you start creating content.

Step #7: Start creating content.

Be it in the form of blog posts or videos, you must start creating content asap! Work closely with your SEO person here and make sure to share everything you post across all your social media, using niche-specific tags where you can.

Step #8: Monetize your niche website.

Monetizing your website is the point of the whole thing. Even if you have huge traffic and millions of social shares, there will be no show for it. There are lots of ways to monetize your website but the easiest ones are via being an **affiliate** or running **display ads**.

- **Monetizing through affiliate offers.** One of the hassle-free ways to generate profit for your new site is through affiliate sales. This is because you can target buyer intent keywords with maximum conversion rates and don't have to deal with customer service. Affiliate links can be added to your website as banner ads, images, or as hyperlinked text in your blog.

Also, you can set up various channels of income with ease and even use affiliate marketing to springboard to new opportunities in the long run.

- **Monetizing through display ads.** With display ads, all you need to do is apply with an ad network, like Google AdSense, so that other businesses can run display ads on your website – which will make a profit for you. 85% of viewers are okay with contextual ads, so don't feel wary about putting up ads on your website. There are several benefits to running hands on your website, such as the fact that you can monetize every page of your site. Your income as an ad promoter can even win over your affiliate income drastically since it can show up on affiliate and non-affiliate content.
- **Start making and promoting products.** A product can be created by any website for sale. However, the most important thing is to create a product that will interest your audience. An easy way to go about this is to discover which of your affiliate products are selling best. Then, you can create a competing product to achieve maximum profit. Nothing is stopping you from selling your products on your site and recommending them as number #1. All you

have to do is take the leap, and the sky will be your limit.

- **Monetization through email marketing.** There are a couple of ways to make money through email marketing. The most common way is to use email marketing to send your audience the content you want them to see - just make sure that content leads to some kind of sale being prompted. With email marketing, you need to build a concrete relationship with your reader/audience before expecting them to purchase anything from you. This relationship is established when you help your readers find solutions to the things they want. Free incentives are always a great relationship builder if you're wondering how to best go about it.

And there you have it! These are the basic steps and requirements for setting up and monetizing your niche website. It is important to note that you can't perform magic overnight. With consistent effort and determination, you can eventually get to your goal…just make sure to start now!

BUILDING NICHE SITES VS AUTHORITY SITES

Now, you may be wondering "what is an Authority Site?" and "why do I see this term go hand-in-hand with niche websites"? Let's get down to clarifying that:

> An **Authority Site** includes the same things as the niche site but takes it a step further in that it intends to present itself or the owner as an expert in a particular niche.

In summary, an authority site is created to become the major source of information within a selected industry. If you can put a face to it, then *you* are the expert.

In an authority site, a trust-based relationship is built with the audience/reader. When creating an authority site, you should be ready to fish in many waters. That is, you will want various income sources, various monetization methods, and different strategies for growth.

As mentioned earlier, rather than just affiliate marketing alone, you can also earn money via display ads. You can even sell your own products whether physical, digital, or even both. Similarly, authority sites try to get traffic from as many sources as possible like Google, social media, podcasts, and email. Since authority sites are large, complex, and very profitable, it is wise to put in great effort to build it for a productive and profitable outcome.

Now let's look at the **pros of an Authority Site:**

- ✔ It is easier to divert into similar niches.
- ✔ Extremely high-income ceiling.
- ✔ Variety of income is more reliable than sole income.
- ✔ You are not prone to a single traffic source.
- ✔ Returning audience.
- ✔ Lucrative exit opportunities.

And what about **the cons?** Let's look at those too:

- Extremely higher than the initial investment.
- Needs long planning.
- Have to wait for a long while to earn profit.
- Requires competitive keywords.
- Much more hands-on business.

When **compared to niche websites**, which has more potential and offers a better return on investment? Which is easier to operate and control? These and more are the questions that will be answered in the comparison table below:

Niche Sites	Authority Sites
Niche sites are generally **smaller in size and following.**	Niche sites are generally **larger in size and following,** but you will often get the little guy making a big impact as well.
Low competition keywords are needed here.	**High competition keywords** are needed to build your audience.
Many niche sites don't grow up past a **hundred posts** that revolve exclusively around a **single topic**.	An authority site can have **thousands of posts** that can branch into **secondary niches.**
Branding a niche site is mostly all about stating what your niche is. So, your website name may be **product-based** and will contain the same match keyword.	**Branding an authority site** should be **more professional.** Including a keyword in the name is cool, but you want your readers to see more value in your brand than just that.
All traffic for niche sites originates **from Google** and occasionally **social media.**	**Multiple channels of reliable traffic** are needed for an authority site.
Most niche sites monetize using **Amazon Associates.**	While some authority sites use Amazon, many others **change their affiliate programs.**
With the niche site, your main **investment is your time,** this is because the domain and hosting cost ranges from 30-100 dollars per year.	With the authority site, **more significant investment is required**. You should expect to spend a couple of thousand dollars in the first year of creating the site because of management and running costs.
A great niche site can make **thousands of dollars** per month.	An authority site can make **hundreds of thousands** per month.

Our chapter on Niche Websites must now come to an end. But I have more ideas on products to sell on such websites in the following chapters...

6

SELF-PUBLISHING BOOKS

Now, I promised you that I have more product ideas to share with you which you can add to your niche website to make a profit from. But when it comes to selling books, there are more platform options and wider audiences you can reach. For example, **Amazon**...

Ask yourself the question: would you rather post your book on your niche website or the largest marketplace in the world?!

No matter where and how you elect to sell your book, there are **many benefits** to be had by getting a book out there, such as:

✔ Making passive income from book royalties for as long as you're alive
✔ Being perceived as an expert in your industry
✔ Connecting and collaborating with other authors and experts
✔ Being able to market other products/services within your books
✔ Growing a loyal fan and customer base who will be eagerly expecting your next books or product

….and more!

But let's start with the very basics, like what self-publishing actually is and how it differs from traditional publishing.

THE WORLD OF SELF-PUBLISHING: GETTING STARTED

To understand self-publishing, you must first get acquainted with the traditional way of publishing a book.

Traditional publishing goes a bit like this: You write a book, then find an agent, who in turn will score you a publishing deal (if you're lucky). Once you sign a contract with the publisher, you receive an advance (usually between $10k-$20k these days) and then expect to get paid in royalties for as long as your book sells. These royalties equate to often no more than 20% of the book's profits.

In essence, the publisher does most of the work for you, hence why they get such a huge cut.

Self-publishing, on the other hand, is the method of publishing a book by yourself. This also implies that you find the tools and resources to edit, format, design and market the book on your own at your own expense.

And there are quite a few **benefits to self-publishing**:

- ✔ You have full control over what you publish and how you publish it.
- ✔ You get to keep most of the royalties (these can reach to over 70%, depending on where and how you publish the book).
- ✔ You can write about anything you want.
- ✔ You aren't pressured by deadlines and other restraints of traditional publishing.
- ✔ You can choose the platform that best suits you, or even multiple platforms.
- ✔ You can outsource most of the work required, which makes the process less stressful and more streamlined.

✔ You can build a fanbase and directly engage with it.

✔ You are in charge of your own marketing, launches, promotions and any events associated with your book.

✔ Writing a book once and having it sell for years to come is a form of passive income. You may even be able to retire off of your backlist, if you have enough books that people enjoy to read.

Let's look at both traditional and self-publishing side by side:

Traditional Publishing	Self-Publishing
As an author, you would require an **agent** and a **publisher**.	You, as the author, are **your own publisher**, no agents or gatekeepers required.
Plenty of **rejection experiences** until you land a publishing deal.	**No rejection or time wasted** on manuscript submissions.
No upfront costs (the publisher funds the entire process).	**Upfront costs** are involved, at **the author's own expense.**
Traditional book sales are a form of **passive income.**	Self-published book sales are a form of **passive income.**
Royalties for the author usually range between **10%-20%** of the book's profits.	Royalties for the author-publisher usually range between **70%-100%** of the book's profits (Amazon also provides a 35% option for those authors wanting to price their books at higher rates).
The publisher will set the author **deadlines** and work on a **strict timeline.**	The author-publisher is **not pressured** by time, deadlines, or any strict timelines.
The author has **little to no control or input** regarding the creative production of their book.	The author-publisher has **full control** over all creative processes and production associated with their book.
The publisher **may create a website for you** (though, these days, most publishers expect the author to already have some kind of platform before submitting their work to them).	You, as the author-publisher, are responsible for **creating your own website, social media, email marketing service, author pages** (Amazon, Goodreads, etc) and any other necessary platform.
As distribution is handled by the publisher, your book will be **available both online and in actual bookstores.**	While it is **easy to sell your book online**, you will need to put in some extra effort and **collaborate with the right distribution company** to get your book into actual stores.
The author is required to **participate in marketing efforts**, events, book signings, etc.	**You, as the author-publisher, devise your own marketing plan** and you are fully responsible for its implementation.

Assuming you would prefer to go the self-publishing route, let's look at what **the process** would entail:

1. Start writing a first draft of your book. Alternatively, you can have a ghostwriter do the work for you.
2. Revise the book and produce a second draft.
3. Find an editor to whom you will give the second draft.
4. In the meantime, you can locate a book cover designer and a formatter.
5. When the manuscript is ready, get it formatted internally. If you plan to turn it into an eBook, this will be formatted differently compared to a print book.
6. Get the designer to design your cover. A back cover and spine will also be required if you plan to have a printed version of the book, too.
7. For the print version, a blurb will also be required, so make sure to either write that yourself or hire a copywriter to do it.
8. If you are working with a copywriter, get them to also write the sales copy (book description) that will accompany the book on the website it will be on.
9. Upload your book on Amazon or another retailer, along with all necessary files, images,

and sales copy. A self-publishing company like IngramSpark is another way to get your book on various platforms. You can even include your book in PDF format on your own website, or simply by adding a link to Amazon where it can be purchased from.

But how much will all this cost you? On average, you can expect to pay anywhere between $500 to $2,000 to self-publish a book these days. Here is a breakdown of **the main self-publishing costs** you should be aware of:

Professional publishing services	Cost
Book editing	$300 - $1500
Book formatting	$30 - $200
Book interior design	$50 - $200
Cover design	$100 - $700
Blurb and copywriting services	$30 - $60 per copywriting hour

Do, however, keep in mind that the above costs do not include the **purchase of an ISBN** (as this is not mandatory to sell a book) or any **advertising efforts** you may elect to implement — it's entirely up to you how much you will be spending on that, if you want to tackle it all it.

Now, once you have written your book and invested time and money on its design and finalization, you would have to put it up for sale, correct? We mentioned

Amazon, but there are other platforms to keep in mind as well. Let's take a look and compare **the main platforms self-publishers use**:

- **Amazon:** It's the number #1 destination for books, as well as the world's top marketplace for all sorts of goods. It also dominates the self-publishing space, as over 80% of the current eBook market is housed under it. For selling your own self-published books, it's a fairly straightforward process: you would just need to sign up for Amazon KDP and select your royalty plan (35% or 70%).
- **Apple iBooks:** Coming right after Amazon, Apple's iBook is gaining more and more traction in the self-publishing sphere. As a self-published author, you can expect to earn 70% in royalties, however your books can only be read via an Apple/Mac device.
- **Barnes & Noble:** Like Amazon, this major bookstore also functions as a self-publishing platform, Barnes & Noble Press (formerly known as NOOK Press) where you can upload your book files and sell as you would through Amazon. Royalties range from 40% to 70%.
- **Kobo:** This is go-to platform for those self-published authors looking to access an

international market. Through Kobo, you can make your book available to Canada plus 190 more countries, and your royalties will depend on how you price your book.

Now, the question remains...what kind of books work best, in terms of format, category and profitability, when it comes to self-publishing?

EBOOKS VS PRINT BOOKS VS AUDIOBOOKS

Let's look a little deeper into the types of books to sell and what you can expect to make from each. You have three options as far as format is concerned:

- eBooks
- Print books
- Audiobooks

eBooks are digital books. They can be read by using an eReader like a Kindle device. Oftentimes, eBooks come in the form of PDFs, which means they can be read on a screen through a desktop computer, laptop or smartphone. Most eBooks can be bought through Amazon's Kindle store, Apple iBooks, and Barnes & Noble.

The benefits of eBooks are:

✔ The lack of a physical object; this enables portability and ease of access to it.
✔ They consume very little data.
✔ They are more affordable than print books.
✔ An entire eBook library can exist on a person's eReader, laptop or phone.
✔ The adjustable font size.
✔ Their built-in dictionary.
✔ The ability to take notes and highlight text.
✔ They are eco-friendly, as paper is not used to produce them.

Print books, on the other hand, are books that are printed and that come in a paperback or hardback binding. These can be sold on online bookstores like Amazon as well as brick-and-mortar stores like Barnes & Noble (USA, Canada) and Waterstones (UK).

The benefits of print books are:

✔ They can be touched, felt, smelled and enjoyed by readers who want a real, sense-based book experience.
✔ They can be produced as a paperback, hard-back, even as a limited edition leatherbound.

✔ They are sought after by collectors and book-worms alike.
✔ They are still high in the market (and often outsell eBooks), despite being tangible products in the age of digitalization.

Audiobooks, lastly, are audio files of a book that can be listened to on any acoustic device. They can be created on ACX (Audiobook Creation Exchange) by which they can then be sold on Amazon's Audible platform.

The benefits of audiobooks are:

✔ They are highly convenient for people on the go.
✔ They take the stress off excessive reading, which is a great benefit for students.
✔ They improve listening skills and the ability to retain information.
✔ They help some people sleep, relax, and improve their mental health.
✔ They are affordable, as are the plans that include unlimited access to them.
✔ Their portability.
✔ A person can listen to more books per year than they can read.

In my humble opinion, you should be targeting all three of these formats. But we can't fully delve in strategy in this book alone (and you're still a beginner here) and would much rather give you some statistics at this point so that you can gauge the potential for each format yourself:

eBooks	Print books	Audiobooks
25% of US consumers read an eBook in 2019.	65% of US consumers read a print book in 2019.	20% of US consumers listened to an audiobook in 2019.
eBook sales increased 16.5% in 2020.	Print books sold twice as many units in 2020 compared to eBooks (USA, UK, Germany).	The average number of audiobooks listened to per year increased to 8.1 in 2020, up from 6.8 in 2019.
7% of Americans say they only read eBooks.	In a 2019 survey, 65% of readers said they picked up a print book in the previous year. 37% of Americans claim they only read print books.	In a 2019 survey, 20% had listened to at least one audiobook.
eBook revenue in 2020 was $956 million in total.	Print books generated 74.7% of the total revenue in 2019.	Audiobook revenue has been up 14.3% year-over-year. In 2020, audiobooks in the US were a 1.3 billion dollar industry.

As you may be able to deduce, print books are still quite popular (thanks to the Covid-19 pandemic) while audiobooks are on a substantial rise. The audiobook market is also a fairly untapped into, if you consider that there are less than 300,000 audiobooks published thus far (November 2021) compared to nearly 50 *million* books on Amazon. That's a **big gap in the market** with some huge potential right there!

And the book business in general is only expected to grow. The global book market is projected to surge from approximately $90 billion in 2021 to $124.2 billion in 2025!

TYPES OF BOOKS TO SELL: FICTION, NON-FICTION, LOW-CONTENT

Now, you may be wondering: "That's all fine and dandy, but what should I even be publishing content-wise in the first place?". That's a great question and while providing an answer that applies to everyone is a challenge, I will aim to offer you some guidance on what each category is renowned for and how bestselling status is normally attained per category.

Let's look at fiction, nonfiction and low-content books:

Fiction books are based on non-factual narratives. This category sells really well if you're either an already famous author or you self-publish rapidly under certain genres. The romance genre is currently dominating the self-published fiction market. On Amazon in particular, self-published fiction equates to 30% of the daily revenue acquired, while the bigger publishers earn the 70%.

Thing to know before self-publishing fiction:

- You would probably need to start with a popular genre if you want to see any kind of revenue — or splurge out on elaborate marketing and advertising if you choose another.
- Acquiring a fanbase is of utmost importance when it comes to fiction. This means you should be ready to engage on social media, network at book festivals and events, and even potentially collaborate with other authors and their fans.
- "Rapid release" is the most common way to publish fiction these days, that is if you're looking for a consistent fanbase and earnings. Readers get bored and forget authors who take their time to publish the next book.
- You are always competing against the big publishers, which can be rather daunting.

Non-fiction books are based on real events, stories or facts. This category is smaller market than fiction, but it is also less competitive and highly lucrative. Non-fiction makes up only 30% of eBook sales, but 50% of that market is dominated by independent self-publishers. It's a great option for entrepreneurs, business owners, consultants, founders, and industry experts of all sorts, as a non-fiction book is practically a "business card" and a way to show off your expertise through providing valuable content. Self-Help is one of the most popular nonfiction sub-categories here.

Things to know before self-publishing non-fiction:

- You should not publish a non-fiction book unless you already have some kind of online presence. No one wants to read a book written by a digitally invisible author.
- Books that do well in this category are the ones that contain highly practical and useful content ("How-To's" are all the rage here).
- Targeting keywords that are popular and have low competition is the best way to get your book seen and purchased.
- You can treat your book as a lead magnet, adding links to other products and services within it.
- You can sell your non-fiction book directly from your website, particularly if it's a shorter book or PDF and your website generates some good niche-specific traffic.

Low-Content books are just that: books with very little content inside them. These include journals, guest books, diaries, planners, coloring books, etc. Tackling this market is a good option for those who want to spend more time coming up with original and creative ideas rather than writing thousands of words.

Things to know before self-publishing low-content:

- You should have some kind of creative flair before entering this market (most of the time, it's the cover design and wording on it that compels the customer to purchase).
- There is a lot of competition in this market, so sloppy covers and bad interiors won't cut it (unless they are remarkably original!). Hence, if you're not the designer type, you should consider outsourcing this part of the process to someone who is (you can, in fact, outsource the entire production process while you focus solely on generating the next big low-content book idea).
- Customizable low-content books also do well in this market as do books that can be given as gifts, but you would most likely have to sell them on platforms like Etsy and Ebay.

And there you have it: a comprehensive breakdown on what each book category can achieve and what you should be aware of prior to delving into each.

THE SECRETS TO MARKETING YOUR SELF-PUBLISHED BOOK

So, you wrote the book, uploaded it to Amazon, and now you're expecting those dollar signs to roll in. Well…it doesn't really happen that way. You've got to know a thing or two about marketing books first – perhaps even while you are still in the writing phase.

Book marketing is a field which all self-published authors must take seriously — even if you don't think you're cut out for it. The marketing phase of your book is the most delicate stage of each publishing project, and it is also the phase in which results can be highly variable. It's additionally a very learnable process, even for beginners, and one that even seasoned authors learn from continuously. Once you find the tools and methods that work for you, it may become a piece of cake sooner than you think.

Unlike traditionally published authors (who still need to do a lot of promotion themselves, mind you), you are the one who will decide on your marketing plan and how much effort, time and money you want to invest into it.

In order to reach new readers through your marketing, you have to set up a precise and long-term strategy.

Let's take a look at the basics of **how to promote a book successfully**:

1. Offer a quality product
2. Attract
3. Put the reader at the center

Let's now look deeper into these three crucial steps:

1. Offer a quality product

Every book, in general, must be a quality product. But if it is a self-published book, this becomes imperative. Why? Because a self-published book is competing against traditionally published books which are more visible, more accessible and, often wrongly, known as "better quality" books. Your self-published book must therefore be nothing short of high-quality and not offer less than books published by the big publishing houses.

2. Attract

You can do marketing in two ways: by pushing the *product* toward customers or by attracting customers *to* the product. This is the difference between what is known as "push and pull marketing".

Doing *push marketing* means putting your book in front of the eyes of uninterested customers and insisting that they buy it. Generally, all the commercials that we see on television are a type of push marketing, proposing a product that most viewers are not even looking for. In this case, the skill of the advertisers lies in presenting the product to them, making them appreciate its characteristics, and instilling in those viewers the desire to own that product.

Pull marketing means attracting customers ALREADY interested in the topic, talking about the product, intriguing them, and convincing them to buy.

3. Put the reader at the center

When you write, there is only you and a blank page; it is you who sets the pace, rhythms, structure, tone, and so on, to create your unique manuscript. When it comes to publishing, on the other hand, you need to get more technical about things and address that manuscript – your book-to-be – as a physical product: you set it up, format it, design it, and upload your files on various online marketplaces. Hence, publishing is less about you and more about the product (book).

Then we have promotion, which is all about the reader. It is no longer an intimate and private matter that concerns only you as a writer and it is not a technical phase that deals with the book as a product.

To promote a book, you have to put yourself on the reader's side and imagine what they think, what they like and don't' like, and what influences their choices. It's a fundamental change of perspective, but if you are a reader before being a writer, it shouldn't be difficult to change perspective and adopt the right point of view.

Now, you may have heard of the term *funnel* before in marketing, and I want to

---

A **funnel** is a sales model that involves several stages of customer engagement with a brand, from the point of having little to no awareness of it, to purchasing the brand's product or service.

I want to outline a very basic funnel process for you to get acquainted with. It is structured through four descending stages your potential customer goes through, known by the acronym AIDA:

- A for Attention;
- I for Interest;
- D for Desire;
- A for Action.

A for Attention

A prospective customer must first become aware of your product or even just you as an author. You can initially capture their attention on social media, your own site or blog, or via paid advertising directly on platforms such as Amazon.

> ➢ **Expert tip:** If you're aiming to break through as a brand-new author, and if your budget can handle it, start with an ad on social media or Amazon. Just make sure you are already somewhat active online prior to doing this.

I for Interest

Readers show interest in their favorite authors. So how can you become theirs? In terms of your social presence, readers will follow you on social media, read your articles and posts, and interact with you if your content is interesting (personal photos or book cover reveals, for instance). They also show interest when they see a new post or product of yours. When it comes to ads, there must be something in the visual that will intrigue them to want to learn more about your book.

> ➢ **Expert tip:** Make sure your ad or post or whatever you are using to attract the potential

customer includes an interesting design or wording that elicits curiosity (for example, "The No-BS Online Business Model No One Is Talking About...REVEALED in My Latest Book!").

D for Desire

Once the prospective customer is curious, they will not hesitate to move onto the next step: that of desiring what you have to offer. Instilling that sense of desire and convincing them that they need what you have to offer can be done via an ad, an email campaign, or social media as long as you have already been building a relationship with that prospect.

> ➢ **Expert tip:** Give your prospect something they will absolutely want, rave about, and can attain easily, something that is ideally also useful and free (a sneak-peek of the first few chapters of your book, for example).

A for Action

The prospective customer's action is to buy your book, sign up for a sample of it, join your mailing list, or take some kind or initiative based on a call to action (CTA). At this final stage in the funnel, you will have sifted through those whose attention you grabbed, those interested in learning more about you/your book, and those who have desired your product, only to end up with a few willing to spend money to buy your book or sign up. That's what it's called a *funnel.*

Think about how many times you have been struck by an ad or a piece of news and have found yourself interested in a particular product. Perhaps you looked up information, ratings and prices, maybe you even went to a store to try it on, and maybe you even waited 'til you had enough funds to purchase it. All in all, you went through various stages of the prospect's journey, and only at the end did you brave to make the purchase.

Every prospective customer behaves this way; As a seller, you should always keep the customer journey in mind and create all your funnels around it. Knowing the mechanism that moves the choices of those who buy helps you pinpoint how to act when you find yourself on the seller's side.

As an author who wants to promote their books, your goal must be to get noticed and attract the attention of as many potential readers as possible: the more people you can get into the funnel, the higher the number of prospects who will reach the end of the funnel and buy your book.

The funnel example touched a lot on advertising and social media. But let's now look into some other **powerful book-marketing methods**:

- Amazon Advertising (if you publish trough KDP)
- Press releases
- Communities
- Interviews (on blogs, channels and podcasts)
- Literary contests
- Discounts, giveaways and promotions
- ARCs

➢ Amazon Advertising

Among the paid promotion methods, Amazon Ads is the best in cost/performance ratio. That's because Amazon is basically a search engine. Unlike Google or Facebook, when a user connects to Amazon this user is already searching for a book.

Amazon Ads deserve their own chapter (as advertising deserves its own book), so I'll simply give you some pointers her on how to get the most out of your ads without wasting a ton of money on them:

- Search the competition first, particularly bestselling titles in your category, even if they are by unknown authors.
- Understand how Amazon Advertising works and how ads are priced (so that you can budget accordingly). What determines the cost of your ads, the number of impressions, and the likelihood of clicks and conversions is not the budget but the bid for each individual target.
- If you want to appear next to a famous book in that competition, your bid will have to be higher, so do be realistic about what you can afford.
- When creating your ad, make sure to narrow down your chosen category as much as possible. For example, let' say you have chosen "thrillers and suspense". You can then select “refine” and select a subcategory under “genre”.
- It would be best to find the right keywords for any Amazon Ad promotion to work efficiently.
- It's not so much about finding keywords relevant to your book's topic but finding keywords that the potential customer can type in. If the two match, all the better.
- Don’t be afraid of trial and error. Test out keywords and price ranges until you strike that perfect balance.

- Don't do guesswork — use tools to help you. You can make use of software that searches for keywords, such as Helium10 (which you can install as a Chrome browser add-on), or Amalyze AG.

➢ Press Releases

One of the easiest ways to promote your book is to write and distribute press releases. Unfortunately, many authors ignore or snub this marketing method because they think it has gone out of fashion and that, in the age of the Internet, a press release no longer has any value.

But they're wrong. In fact, press releases are one of the easiest ways to promote your book because they require very little effort to write and distribute. Moreover, you can write them yourself and disseminate them for free in many dedicated portals. It is, therefore, a no-cost book marketing tool. So why not take advantage of it?

➢ Community

Being present in reader groups and actively participating in them is another effective way to market your book. After all, before being a writer you were certainly a reader and therefore know from experience that, to choose which new titles to read, you take into great consideration the reading recommendations that come from people you know or trust. We all read books because someone recommends them to us, and the advice is all the more convincing the more friendly the person giving it to us is.

But you shouldn't enter such communities with a salesy "I'm-here-to-sell-my-books" approach. Rather, make the purpose for attending reader communities more about finding new friends and people with whom you can exchange reading recommendations.

- **Interviews (on blogs, channels and podcasts)**

If being in the public eye doesn't scare you, you can connect with bloggers, YouTube channel owners and podcasters for interview opportunities. In many cases, the author interviewed offers an exchange for the free publicity, such as promoting the blog, channel or podcast themselves on their social media or their own website.

➢ Literary contests

Only writers, published or unpublished, can enter writing contests, which makes this a unique-to-authors marketing method. This is a great way to get seen by not only your peers and potential readers, but also agents and publishers alike. Some literary competitions require that you send them a book that has already been self-published, which is a fantastic book visibility boost!

➢ Discounts, giveaways and promotions

Offering frequent discounts and giveaways is a wonderful way to promote not only your current book but also your backlist. Got an old book that isn't selling anymore? Have it on sale or bundle it up with another book as special discounted offer!

And that wraps up our self-publishing chapter. But do keep in mind the following: When you're selling books, you're essentially selling content — and content can come in various shapes, sizes and formats. In the next chapter, I will reveal just one more of those formats.

7

SELLING ONLINE COURSES

We addressed self-published non-fiction books as a means of providing industry-specific information that is valuable, useful and applicable. That same information can be used (and even repurposed) to **create online courses**.

Launching online courses is a highly sought-after business model these days. For starters, online learning has actually grown considerably since the global pandemic of 2020-2021. People want to learn more, and have the time to do so, particularly through self-paced bite-sized digitalized lessons and video format.

Though developing an online course does take some time and effort, the end result may astound you. Many course creators manage to make passive income from their courses for years, not to mention live off of their revenue full-time.

Fortunately for you, releasing an online course does not need to be challenging. With the aid of this book, you are going to discover crucial elements of an effective online course release and the very first stepping stones required to get you there.

WHY SELL ONLINE COURSES?

Now, you may be thinking: Why should I even consider developing an online course?

Let me turn that question around: Why shouldn't you, if you have something great to share with others? It can be anything from a simple DIY or craft project, like how to restore old furniture or crochet, to how to set up an online business, speak Italian, or learn reflexology.

But let's look at some of the actual **benefits of selling online courses**:

- ✔ **Highly profitable, if you do it right**

The best thing about offering an online course is that you can make moderate to huge profit, if you play your cards right — that translates to providing useful content that is well-presented, well-marketed and in high demand while appealing to a niche group of customers that are happy to spend their money on it.

✔ A great passive income stream

With online courses, you create and publish the course once and have it up for sale for as many years as you want. You don't need to put any extra legwork into it, except for maybe putting up and ad every now and then and updated the course's content if it seems outdated.

✔ A real reputation builder

Offering an online course enables you to produce a name for yourself, get known in the industry, and earn the trust of both your peers as well as those who want to learn from you.

✔ It's practically marketing

Just a book can be your "business card", so can an online course be your stamp of authority and proof of your qualifications. It can also function as part of your marketing funnel and a gateway to your actual business. For example, if you are a designer teaching people how to create a logo, they will eventually visit your design agency website and may even purchase a full website or branding package from you.

If you're sold on the benefits and can't wait to learn more about setting up your own online course, I want you to first ask yourself: Who are you as a course creator?

ARE YOU AN EXPERT, EXPERIENCER OR MESSENGER?

When thinking about creating an online course, you should ideally start with some self-inspection and recognize what type of individual you are. If you have a PhD then it probably makes sense to think you are an expert on your studied topic. But what if you never went to university?

Here is a **sequence of questions** to ask yourself if you *don't* have a PhD and are struggling to figure out your credentials as a course creator:

- Am I enthusiastic and well-versed on a specific subject?
- Am I extremely skilled, experienced or knowledgeable on a specific subject?
- Is this subject something I love talking about and advising on often?

- Would I like to assist other individuals in learning more about this subject, skill or ability?
- Would I still teach individuals the how-to's of this subject even if I wasn't earning any money? Would I still enjoy doing it for free?

If you replied with "yes" to at least 3 of these questions, then developing an online course is most definitely suitable for you! And I wouldn't spend a minute disputing or questioning that — PhD or not!

So then, how would you go about creating the course? How would you present yourself to the world? I like to think of course creators in three categories: Experts, Experiencers and Messengers:

An **Expert** is usually officially qualified and has studied their craft or subject academically. They have at least one degree and may be accredited or licensed via organizations within their sector (for example, you haven't just earned a Master's in Psychology, but you are actually a licensed psychologist).

An **Experiencer** doesn't need a degree or official qualification. They know what they know due to their experience. For example, someone who has been gardening organically for over 20 years is well-experienced in the subject and practice and could very well create a course on "Getting Started with Organic Gardening" for complete beginners.

A **Messenger** is usually neither a degree-holder nor a person with years of experience in a particular topic, craft or practice. But what this person does have is a deep interest and passion for the subject they teach. They also get a real thrill out of learning as much as they can about it. Perhaps they've read a ton of books on the topic or have attended a lot of courses to the point that they can convey the content that they've learned so well. They might also be avid researchers who just love to relay their findings.

So, ask yourself: Are you an Expert, and Experiencer or a Messenger? Use the following table to help you make that decision:

	Expert	Experiencer	Messenger
FOCUS	Your **official qualifications** in the subject at hand.	Your **years of experience** in the subject at hand.	Your years of pursuing **knowledge and learning** about the subject at hand.
CONTENT	**Academically-sourced content** without the academic jargon (must be as **beginner-friendly** as possible, unless you are addressing other academics).	First-person, **experience-based content**, as students will want to learn from your own hands-on knowledge, trials and errors.	**A mix** of first and third-person content (as you will want to **quote experts**).
BEST FORMAT	**Video-based courses** or a combination of video and **textual syllabus. Audio** also works well here.	**Video-based courses** or **live workshops.** Some helpful **templates,** images and textual material is also highly appreciated (as long as its practical).	**Any kind of format** will do, but **video content** will build more trust and authority. To convince others of your expertise, you might want to go the extra mile with your syllabus (video, text, image, live workshops and audio).
NICHES THAT DO WELL	Self-help, health, fitness, nutrition, beauty, life/ business coaching, technology, finance, business, law, humanities, science, languages.	Business, marketing, home and garden, beauty, DIY, crafts, repairs, tech, creative arts, spirituality, music.	Any topic that you don't need an official qualification/license to advise on (like a medical or law degree).

Now that you have hopefully been encouraged to create a course based on your expertise, no matter how that has been acquired, let's take a deep dive into platforms that can house that course.

COURSE PLATFORMS VS YOUR OWN WEBSITE

At this point, you should be asking yourself which is the best option for selling your course: Should you sell it on your own website or another platform? While both options are extremely efficient, they each have their own benefits and disadvantages.

Selling Your Course on Online Course Platforms

Pros: Selling a course on a mass online course platform is one of the most convenient ways to launch your online course, especially the first time you try your hand at it. Such platforms take hosting and the overly technical stuff out of the equation, as they are specifically designed to host course content, in all its structures and digital formats (text, eBooks, images, audios, videos). Furthermore, you do not need to invest much to use most of these platforms. Let's have a look at the best ones by name:

- **Udemy**: Udemy is one of the most popular platforms to create and sell your online courses. It has over 18 million students and offers over 45,000 courses on a variety of topics. It's up to you whether you want to offer an online course for free or charge a fee for enrolling on the course. If you decide to charge a fee, Udemy takes a whopping 45% commission from each sale before it gets paid out.

- **Skillshare**: Skillshare is an online learning platform that is very similar to Udemy. It offers online courses mainly for professional or personal development. Skillshare allows you to create your own courses and sell them on their site. Like Udemy, Skillshare takes up to 45% commission from each sale before it gets paid out to you.
- **Teachable**: Teachable is a platform that allows you to create and sell your own online courses. They are geared towards those savvier in course creating and offer branding, marketing and coding options. There's flexibility when it comes to pricing, too: you can offer courses on their own or in bundles, and even choose between a one-time fee, a payment plan, or a subscription.
- **Thinkific**: In a similar vein to Teachable, Thinkific is another great platform for creating and selling branded online courses. You can create your landing page for your course and either build the syllabus within it or import the content from other platforms such as Udemy and Skillshare.

- **Kajabi**: One of the priciest subscription-based options, Kajabi is renowned for its marketing opportunities for busy course creators. Through marketing blueprints known as *Pipelines*, Kajabi helps you create an entire marketing funnel—from the landing page and opt-in to your emails and course checkout!
- **Podia**: Podia is a course publishing website that offers membership payment options to students through a simple, no-fuss digital storefront. Once you create your course, you can publish it immediately or pre-launch it to collect emails. Their payment plans are also quite reasonable.
- **LearnWorlds**: LearnWorlds is a platform that helps you not only create your own course, but your own digital school! Your school can include multiple teachers and a course catalog with various pricing options. You can even get a branded app for your school, for an extra cost.
- **Mighty Netoworks**: This platform gives you the opportunity to build an active, paid community around your course. You can sell individual courses, community memberships, or a bit of both. Course pricing is also rather flexible and 100% custom.
- **Creative Live**: Creative Live is a platform that offers live and on-demand education in

different creative fields such as guitar lessons, photography, makeup artistry and more. It's oriented mostly towards people looking to develop their professional skills.

Cons: The disadvantage of utilizing some of these online course platforms is that you don't have much control over how your courses are presented, paired/bundled, and sometimes even marketed. On Udemy and Skillshare, for instance, you are not able to choose exactly what other people sell along with your course.

Selling Your Course on Your Own Website

Selling an online course on your own website is very rewarding, but it may be more challenging than selling a course on a premade and predesigned online course platform.

Pros: On your own website, you have total control over your courses and can design and market them as you please. You wouldn't have to worry about revenue made based on percentages or any other restrictions.

Cons: Selling your course on your own website implies that you need a website that is well-designed and fully capable of housing your course content or portal. It should also cater for all the techy stuff like enrollments, payments, memberships, syllabus downloads, and the overall accessibility to the course itself. To do this, you can either develop your very own site from scratch or utilize a third-party website builder like Squarespace or Wix.

GROW YOUR REACH, SCALE YOUR BUSINESS

While creating a course is already quite tricky, selling it takes a lot of skill too. I don't want to discourage you here, but the fact of the matter is this: **it takes more than just fantastic content to sell your course**, especially if you have chosen a highly competitive niche. It's the same with books, blogs, and any other form of content that no one will even know exists unless you market it efficiently.

I want to offer you some **tips on how to market your course** and extend its reach to a bigger, more vibrant audience:

1. **Create a mini-course and offer it for free.** This mini-course doesn't have to be too complicated, and it doesn't have to be full of content. Just make sure that it's exciting enough to generate interest from your target audience. You can also create a short introductory course to the main course you have created. This will

entice your customers to continue learning from you and purchase the bigger course.

2. **Find affiliates.** Generate an affiliate link and give it to people who want to promote your course for a commission. As part of your affiliate marketing strategy, you can give other people (even those who have already purchased your course) opportunities to promote your course. In exchange, you offer them rewards like discounts, freebies or, in the case of business owners promoting your courses, you can offer a certain percentage of the amount of each sale.
3. **Write guest posts.** Collaborate with another blogger or business and write for their personal or professional website for free – that's also free exposure and promotion for you. Make sure the platform you choose is owned by influential people in your niche who already have a substantial following. If their followers see your name and guest posts on the website, they will be curious about what you have to offer and check out your work, too.
4. **Attend meetups and local events** (both online and offline) that will give you a chance to meet people in your niche. If you get the chance, you

can even speak at such events to promote your courses.

5. **Host joint webinars.** Team up with well-known people in your industry and host either live or recorded webinars based on what you both teach.
6. **Promote your course on your blog.** Create an article about your course where you explain what it is all about in a fun and exciting way. Don't want to sound too salesy? Then you can simply add a call to action at the bottom of a niche-relevant article or subtly link some relevant text to your course.
7. **Offer discounts and promotional bundles** that include your courses. For instance, if you have created five courses that are similar to each other, you can bundle them and offer them at a lower price for those who will purchase all five. Or you can also offer discounts after your customers have made their first purchase.
8. Find ways to **gamify your course-related content**. Offer challenges, polls, and even mini-games that are related to your course. For example, if your course is on Yoga, why not create a 5-day challenge to practice one sun salutation daily? This is an effective but also fun way to generate interest in your course.

9. **Translate your course in different languages** to make it more versatile. If you can speak different languages, this is a brilliant marketing strategy as you will be extending your courses reach throughout various countries and cultures. If you cannot speak any other language, you can opt to hire a translator to do this for you.
10. **Cross-promote all your courses**. When you have already created several courses, make sure each links or directs to the other so that they are constantly promoting each other.
11. **Optimize your course according to SEO.** Use the best practices here, which include optimizing your course URL, meta description, meta tags, headings, subtitles, blog posts, images and captions according to your chose keywords.
12. **Start your own YouTube channel** where you will introduce your course, publish updates, and even create a course promotion video for when your launch date approaches. You can also connect with other YouTubers and ask them to promote your course on their channels (but you will have to exchange the favor somehow).

13. **Start a podcast or be a guest on one.** Sign up on platforms like Google Play, Stitcher or iTunes then submit podcasts about your course. Creating a podcast or being a guest on one is a great way to let your target audience know who you are while promoting your course and piquing their interest in it.
14. **Create a Facebook page exclusively for your course** (this should be different from your personal Facebook profile). If you plan to create several courses, create a page for your brand where you will post everything related to your courses like advertisements, special offerings, and sneak peeks. You can also take advantage of **Facebook ads** if you want more people to learn about your upcoming courses.
15. **Connect with influencers** on social media and ask them to review your course. Offer them a discount on your course and if they enjoy it, they might even start promoting it!

I hope you are now pumped on creating your first online course and learning as much as you can about what it takes to be successful in this business.

If, on the other hand, you're still on the fence about which business model suits you best, please don't make a decision before you read the final chapter…

8

FREELANCING

According to a study conducted by Upwork, a large freelancing platform provider, about 57 million Americans were freelancing in 2019. If the trend continues, more than half of Americans will be freelancing in the future.

But why am I even discussing freelancing? Doesn't that mean that you will have to provide a service and actually get a lot of work done? What's so passive about that?

By the end of this chapter, you will know how to not only get started with an online freelance business, but how to also **turn it into an automated machine** providing you with at least semi-passive income.

But let's get started with the very basics.

FREELANCING EXPLAINED

Freelancing is a highly sought-after way to earn a living these days. No commuting. No boss telling you what to do. But what is a freelancer and how do they work exactly?

> A **freelancer** is a self-employed person who provides services to clients.

These services are often, though not required, offered to businesses through a proliferation of shared economy platforms such as Freelancer, Fiverr or Upwork. But freelancers can also offer their services directly to customers without the use of third parties who often take a pay cut.

Almost every type of service required by a business can be provided by a freelancer. Some of the most common freelance opportunities include:

- Administration and virtual assistance
- Programming and IT
- Software engineering
- Design (web, graphic and multimedia)
- Marketing and sales

- Accounting and financial consultancy
- Business development and consultancy
- Writing and proofreading/editing
- Legal and paralegal services

Some freelancers focus in general areas while others focus in specific industries and niches, such as real estate virtual assistants or email copywriters.

Freelance income varies depending on the skills you provide, your experience, and the market you target. In general, freelancers earn anywhere from $10 to $75 per hour. Skills that require more education or experience, such as accounting or website coding, usually pay more than skills that don't require as much.

But if you are interested in joining the gig economy and earning money in the context of a full-time job, you must understand the many advantages and disadvantages of this type of income generation.

Advantages of freelancing include:

✔ **A quick and affordable setup.**

You can be up and running as soon as you create your online profile. You won't even have to pay to use such a platform until you start earning income from it.

✔ Working from home.

99% of the time you will not need to commute as a freelancer. It's the ideal way to work from home.

✔ Flexibility.

Freelancing is flexible as you set your own schedule. You can elect to work full-time or part-time on projects of your choice at a time that is convenient for you.

✔ Location independence.

Freelancing is a great portable option for those who want to work from wherever they want. If you love to travel while earning money or live the "digital nomad" lifestyle, then freelancing may be the business model for you.

✔ Setting your own rules.

From contracts to hourly rates, you have considerable control over how you work and charge for it. Although clients can (and usually will) set the specifications for the scope of work they need done, a freelancer is still an independent contractor, and should therefore be able to set up their own contracts or at least suggest terms, as and when needed.

✔ **No need for elaborate or fancy equipment.**

Unless a client requests that you have the latest paid software or a high-performance iMac, you really don't need to go out of your way to purchase equipment. However, this will depend on the services you provide. For instance, a basic laptop with MS Word installed might do wonders for a writer, but may be completely useless for a graphic designer who would require a more professional device to handle heavier software.

✔ **The current (and growing) high demand.**

Although the freelance marketplace is competitive, the need for quality, reliable freelancers is increasing. Many businesses these days don't have employees and instead rely on a team of remote-working freelancers. The trend is currently increasing because freelancers cost less for businesses than employees, even though they pay higher rates—because they don't have to pay payroll fees or benefits.

✔ **You call the shots.**

No one makes decisions for you when it comes to freelancing. You can either accept to decline a project or task depending on your time, commitments, or just plain preference. You also have the option of not taking on difficult clients, especially as you grow. You can also tell clients that you no longer want to work for them at any given time (though, do be aware of any contract terms you may have agreed to).

✔ **You may pay less in taxes.**

The tax office treats employees and independent contractors quite differently. In most countries, independent contractors can deduct expenses from their taxable income, while employees can't.

✔ **Increase in work/life balance.**

Stress little about life and little about work. Isn't that what everyone wants? When you can choose what you do and when to do it, as well as what you get paid and who you work with, you're more likely to feel balanced and happier overall. You can also take time off as and when you need it to spend time with your family, go on a hiatus, travel, focus on your hobbies, recover from illness, or just plain chillax.

Now, let's also look into some of the major **disadvantages of freelancing:**

— **Freelancing isn't for everyone.**

Not everyone is freelancer material or suited for this type of profession long-term. It takes a certain personality to endure the ups and downs of the job along with time management, organization and communication skills.

— **Time zone problems.**

You should always keep time zones in mind when working with a client in another country, especially when they request a Zoom meeting or teamworking hours. You shouldn't accept any offer that requires you to be available during certain hours you aren't able to.

— **Clients can be a drag.**

You may want the job, but what if the client is difficult? What if they take their time to approve your work, thus delaying overall project delivery? Maybe they email or call you often to the point that you lose focus or have to make constant tweaks and changes. While you should be prepared to say "yes" more than "no" when you're first starting out, you must eventually set boundaries and a define your tolerance levels, or clients may end up trampling all over you.

— Unpredictability.

Work is not always consistent in the freelance world. This is especially the case if you are providing one-off services, like designing a website. You finalize your project, deliver to the client, and that's the end — you have to then find a new client and start a new one-off project, and the cycle never ends. Sometimes, workflow can be so unpredictable that you may not even have that next client for weeks, even months. More experienced freelancers can avoid this problem by finding clients who require work consistently; for example, a freelance writer may have a client who needs an article twice a week on an ongoing basis.

— Success takes time.

While you can set up the business fairly quickly and land a quick gig or two, you can't fully succeed overnight as a freelancer. It can take some time to acquire enough clients to support yourself and your family financially, and many freelancers experience ups and downs in their work for years until they reach that stage. This is why you have to be prepared to work hard and deliver projects on time when work is plentiful while putting savings aside for those less busy months.

– **Multitasking.**

Some freelancers love it, while others loathe it. The truth of the matter is that multitasking will crop up at some point (unless you have that one golden client that pays you a consistent full-time income based on a single project). Managing multiple clients as well as multiple projects and their deadlines can be a challenge, so you would constantly have to pace yourself to produce and deliver quality work on time.

– **Competition.**

Most freelance sites are rife with…you guessed it… freelancers! You are often competing with over 20 freelancers on any given job, maybe even 50 or more. Unless you know how to stand out and appeal to your prospective client, landing a job may be excruciatingly hard. You should also be the king of person who doesn't give up easily or gets discouraged when others are competing against you.

— You are a business owner.

While this could very well be an undeniable advantage, it also includes a lot of responsibility and a skillset that not all people possess or are comfortable with, particularly newbies. Invoicing, bookkeeping and marketing are all part of the freelancing business. Unless you can hire people to take care of these tasks for you, you need to take care of them on top of delivering your services.

— No benefits.

As a self-employed business owner, you will be deprived of benefits (such as employer-sponsored healthcare) and retirement plans – at least in most countries.

— Self-employment tax.

This is the flipside of paying taxes on low income. When you work for someone else, your employer pays half of your Medicare and Social Security taxes, but when you're independent, *you* are your employer—

meaning you have to pay both. This is commonly known as the self-employment tax.

Are you still with me? Or are you discouraged by the disadvantages? Because this book is all about being real and honest about online business so that you don't learn things the hard way. Yes, there are cons, but the pros can significantly overweigh them if you really want them to.

So, without further ado, let's look into how you can practically and realistically get started with this business model…and succeed!

HOW TO START WORKING AS A FREELANCER

Getting started as a freelancer can be as simple as visiting one of the freelance websites to find work, or networking in your current sphere of influence to locate your first client.

When it comes to working online, you would want to consider using freelance sites rather than cold-calling local prospects and putting ads up in your neighborhood (honestly, who does that these days?). Here are some of the most popular sites freelancers flock to:

- Upwork.com
- Freelancer.com

- Fiverr.com
- Peopleperhour.com

These sites may take a considerable cut (up to 20%) and projects may pay less than you expect, but they are a great way to get your name out there and garner testimonials and referrals as a brand-new freelancer.

In addition to using freelance sites, there are a number of steps you need to take prior to applying for those very first projects:

Step #1: Decide what services you will offer.

What line of work will you be offering? Will you be a generalist or an expert in a particular niche? For example, you can offer social media management across multiple platforms or focus on one, such as Pinterest or Instagram.

Freelance sites like the ones mentioned previously all provide a list of categories you can house your services under. As long as there's a category for what you do, then there is a service and a need for it.

Step #2: Define your target market.

Is there a demand for what you offer? And who are these clients? Where do they live, what businesses do they own, what language do they use and how is their business run and structured? Aim to tackle all these questions until you can clearly visualize your ideal client.

This is also the perfect time to decide on your brand and your unique selling proposition. You may have the skills and experience to sell yourself to large corporations or you may just want to work for small businesses.

Step #3: Set your rates.

Setting the right rate is all about striking that perfect balance between being attractive to clients as well as reflecting your expertise and quality. If you don't charge enough, it may suggest that your work is of little to no value. If you ask for too much, you may not get customers willing to pay those amounts.

You can either charge per project or by the hour. Decide on an acceptable fee per project, as many freelance projects may be one-time gig, in which the client will want to estimate the total job. Other freelancers have ongoing clients who pay a regular rate or retainer. For example, a freelance writer might write eight new articles for a blog for $400 a month, or a virtual assistant might provide 10 hours of work a month for $200.

Step #4: Create an online portfolio.

Create a portfolio that showcases your skills, talent and what you overall have to offer. This can simply be a collection of various work-related files and screenshots or, eventually, you can invest in a website that can offer you more customization and flexibility. You can also showcase your work via LinkedIn, as it's free and functions pretty much like an online resume. You can also consider PortfolioBox, Squarespace and Jarno Portfolio.

But there are underlying systems and principles that go into making a portfolio really stand out in any industry. Ultimately, your portfolio should be created with the intention of appealing to a specific audience of potential clients, sparking their interest and speaking to their needs. To create a client-capturing portfolio that is professional, functional, and illustrative of your skills, I would suggest you **set one up on your own website.** You can use a website builder like Wix, Squarespace or Weebly. Some of these may provide a free domain name along with hosting options, and you can pay a subscription either annually or monthly. Either way, it is definitely worth the investment, and also one of the easiest ways to wow your next client.

Step #5: Get your pro tools in order.

From invoicing tools and contract templates to software you would require to actually work on your projects, you need to now get your freelancer toolkit in order. Don't assume that being on a professional platform will make you a pro. Clients are able to detect a non-professional from the most basic of interactions — especially clients who have been outsourcing projects on freelance websites for years. You might be asked for an invoice, a contract, an official quote/proposal, even something as simple as a business phone number or tax number so do consider all the technical, legal and practical actions you would need to take prior to getting work done.

Step #6: Market your services.

Now that you have a freelance profile and potentially even a website of your own, you need to start promoting yourself. There are quite a few low cost and free ways to market your freelance business and attract clients. Some options include networking on social media, offering free consultations, soliciting referrals, and through email marketing if you already have a list you can work with.

Another way to market yourself as a freelancer is to create content on the topic of your expertise. You can create a blog on your website or write for larger blogs like Medium. YouTube videos can also grant you some visibility, as the platform in the second largest search engine after Google.

You can also consider working for free, just to establish those very first connections and add some further samples to your portfolio. It's totally fine to work for free if you're working for the right people and building substantial professional relationships that may benefit you in the long run and that can open doors to more opportunities. Networking is one of the big secrets to success in this line of work.

SCALE YOUR FREELANCING BUSINESS

You may end up freelancing for years without really growing as a freelancer or scaling your business. You might be earning a steady income month in and month out, but remain oblivious to the amazing potential and growth that can be had in the freelancing business.

I don't want you to end up slaving away as you would in any 9-to-5 job or reaching burnout levels just to be able to make a living as a freelancer, so here are some **growth strategies** you can start implementing, as soon as you're ready to scale your business:

- **Strategy #1: Raise your prices.**

If you want to work less for higher rates, the first thing you can do is increase the pricing of your services. That way, you will lure in quality customers who are willing to pay you more for services that are of higher quality than those priced cheaper. This will give you enough time to focus on these few customers which will lead to more quality work at the end of the day.

- **Strategy #2: Sub-contract.**

If you don't have full-time projects, you may not choose to hire a permanent team, but you can always have other freelancers help you with your larger workloads. You can share projects with them by doing only half or less than half the work yourself. If you trust these freelancers, you can pass entire projects onto them (while you take a considerable cut) especially when you need to travel, focus on other pressing projects or just take some time off.

But where do you find such freelancers? You can either seek out local freelancers, if you're all about helping your local community, or source them online via freelancing websites, just as clients source you! Do note, however, that to do this you would need to set up a client account rather than a freelancer account.

- **Strategy #3: Hire permanent employees.**

You may also decide to permanently hire some workers, locally or remotely, to assist you with certain tasks. This strategy will only work if you are sure that you will always be putting your hired employees working at your desk to good use. If projects aren't stable, it's unwise to have permanent staff that you have to pay weekly or monthly. Therefore, evaluate your options before deciding whether to hire permanently or just sub-contract.

- **Strategy #4: Build and sell through your own platform.**

Freelancing websites have rules that you need to follow if you want to thrive on their platform. Some of these platforms also require you to pay a fee if you want to connect with customers and apply to jobs, not to mention the fact that they also deduct quite a fee for allowing you to use their platform. Wouldn't you rather *not* worry about all that? If you want to grow your freelance business based on *your* rules and yours alone, you have to build your website where prospective clients can visit *you*. It may prove to be challenging at first, particular as you try to figure out how to best promote yourself and get clients to trust you and your work, but it will eventually pay off as you build your reputation.

- **Strategy #5: Build a product.**

You don't need to worry about buying ads to get noticed as a freelancer. Instead, you can create a product which will magnetize clients for you and direct them to your website. For example, if you are a writer, you may consider writing a book and selling it on Amazon. If you are a software developer, you may consider creating an app and putting it up for sale on app sites like Google Play. The point here is to use your skills and experience to build something solid and as passive of an income stream as possible. It can take a while to create a quality product that is useful and in high demand, but once you've made one and it's ready, you won't have to worry about learning the ropes all over again — plus, you have this book to help you get there faster!

TURN FREELANCING INTO A PASSIVE FORM OF INCOME

Scaling a freelance business is one thing, but what about actually turning it into a near or fully passive income stream? How exactly can that be done?

It may seem counterintuitive and a bit nonsensical; you're providing a service, so how the service be provided without you having to put in the hours?

We touched on sub-contracting as a growth strategy. This is the foundation for what I am about to present to you now.

It's what I call the **freelance agency model**. It's still freelancing, but it differs in that:

- Other freelancers do some, most or all the work for you.
- Managers are also hired to oversee the freelancers and relevant operations.
- Client liaisons and a sales team can also be hired, if you would rather not do that either.
- You don't do any work unless you absolutely want to. You can simply focus on management, hiring, client communication, or nothing at all if you have assigned these posts to other freelance managers.
- Regardless of how much work you put it, you will always take a cut out of every project to cover expenses and another to cover your commission. For example, if you charge $1,000 for designing a website, you may want to pay your freelance designer the $700 while assigned

$100 to expenses and the remaining $200 for yourself.

Sounds a bit too good to be true? Let's look at some of the pros and cons of building an agency before you decide whether this business model suits your or not:

Pros	Cons
More free time on your hands (but only if you can afford to hire multiple freelancers to do the work for you).	You may still need to **be in charge of management and finances**, at least in the early stages of the business. This might even **take up more time** that your initial independent freelancer business.
Scalability is limitless. As long as you have projects rolling in, you can hire more freelancers and grow your business as much as you like.	**Limitations** may include a low number of initial clients, budget, and the time required to find goo quality freelancers that you can trust.
Making money passively, without lifting a finger.	While you will be earning passive or semi-passive income, you will still need to **acquire a lot of clients** or at least a few high-paying ones to make full-time income from your commissions.
You can build teams to assist you, such as a sales team, operations team, admin team and management team.	**Teams take time to build**. Not everyone you meet or hire online can be 100% trusted. It takes a lot of time and testing until you find the right people to work with you. You will also need to **be able to afford them** without going bankrupt. For example, no client is paying for your sales team; you are the one who should calculate how much of your earnings should be allocated to covering their wages.
Transparency. With an agency, you are honest about how work is done and outsourced to multiple freelancers. You aren't a freelancer who is slyly sub-contracting to other freelancers while unethically presenting the work as your own.	If you are in any way dishonest about who is getting the work done, **your client might see right through you** and you may risk losing them. Word might also get around and your agency will quickly lose its credibility. If you have **no names or photos of team members on your website,** this might also be a red flag for potential clients, as they won't know who will be doing the work for them and who they can trust.
Agencies are more professional. Clients often perceive agencies as being more professional and well-organized than independent freelancers – and this is usually the truth.	**Agencies can be over-professional, rigid and impersonal.** This is often the case for larger agencies or teams that are still struggling to serve and connect with their clients effectively.
Some clients prefer working with professional agencies, especially if they can handle multiple or diverse aspects of a project (i.e., a full website package consisting of web design, coding, SEO and copywriting).	Some of your clients may still want to **communicate with you directly** rather than go through one of your representatives. If you don't give them the attention they are hoping to get, you may **lose their trust** and even their projects. Other clients **avoid working with agencies** altogether and prefer independent contractors.

If you're ready to jump into creating an online agency, here are the steps I recommend:

Step #1: Start by treating yourself like an agency.

It all begins with the right kind of mentality. This transition from freelancer to agency is first and foremost in your mind. You can honestly make the change starting now: just start using the word "we" as opposed to "I" when interacting with clients, presenting your business, and building a profile or website. Treat yourself and your business and an agency, and that is what clients will treat you as.

> ➢ **Expert tip:** Do also consider using a business name rather than your own name to reflect this change. This might also suggest creating a new legal entity, such as an LLC as opposed to sole proprietorship (no need to make that leap until you are absolutely ready and can count on stable income – agencies can be created by self-employed individuals, too).

Step #2: Create your client pipeline.

Before you can gleefully hop from freelancer to agency, you'll need the revenue to support the transition. If you already have a heftier workload than you can normally handle, then that is a clear sign that it's time to start outsourcing some of it by building your own agency.

Start reaching out to clients, both current, old, and new, and pitch your agency to them. Ideally, you will be focusing on a particular service (writing, design, virtual assistance, social media management, etc) or a particular niche and target audience that service addresses (digital marketing services for health practitioners, editing services for authors, web design for tech and SaaS, etc), so make sure to contact clients that are a perfect fit for that.

> ➢ **Expert tip:** Don't settle for clients that no longer fit your chosen specialism or niche. But don't ignore them either. Instead, tell them of your new services and entice them to check out your new website, should they ever require them. But do be aware: once you have a steady stream of ideal clients, you have to make sure you take extra good care of them.

<u>Step #3:</u> Create products and packages.

A clear offering that follows a distinct process and timeline, and has a certain price, rather than an hourly or vague min to max rate is highly advised. You can also bundle products together and create packages or tiers.

For example, if you offer wiring services, you In order to go from freelance to agency, you'll need to get really good at closing the sale.

> ➢ **Expert tip:** Focus on creating an initial minimal viable product (MVP). Instead of designing all sorts of graphics, you can focus specifically on logo design. Instead of writing all sorts of content and copy, you can focus specifically on email copy. This service can then be turned into a product and priced accordingly.

Step #4: Set up your systems.

Systems, particularly automated ones, will become the bread and butter of your agency business. If they don't, then you will need to do more work manually and on your own — possibly even more than you are cut out for! From handling emails, invoices and orders to onboarding new clients and pitching to prospective ones, you have a substantial array of tasks that can be managed by either teams or software (or a bit of both).

> ➢ **Expert tip:** Software that will streamline core processes associated with your agency business include:

- Project management software
- Email automation software
- Invoicing and financial software
- Client onboarding software
- Customer management software
- Analytics and marketing software

Step #5: Hire people.

There are two types of professionals you should start hiring, or at least considering, if you're serious about your agency business:

- **Freelance workers:** These are the people who will be carrying out most if not all of the service-based work for you: designers, coders, content writers, copywriters, marketers, SEO specialists, social media managers and any kind of professionals that you can assign the bulk of your clients' work to.
- **Freelance managers and administrators:** These people will be handling tasks that are outside of the scope of client projects; they are rather tasks related to your business and even you directly. Some of these people will be overseeing the freelancers and their operations (operation managers, project managers, managing editors), others will be handling

administrative tasks (admins, virtual assistants) while others, if you choose to, will be in charge of sales and marketing (marketing managers, sales reps).

➢ **Expert tip:** You must also **consider yourself!** Consider your input and how you will be contributing to the agency. Will you be in charge of any management or admin tasks? Will you be pitching to clients and communicating projects to your teams? Or will you sit back and let others do all of the work? To make that decision easier, I would encourage you to look at your projects and the consistency of revenue — how much of those earnings can you allocate to freelancers and how much would they have to work for per hour or project so that you too can get a decent cut?

Step #6: Schedule and execute.

It's now time to get to work! But make sure that your freelancers and teams are well aware of how they should work, when to work, the full scope of their work, what is expected of them and when their deadlines are. If you have hired a manager or two, you won't have to worry too much about this step.

> ➢ **Expert tip:** Keep (digital) project calendars and logs of every project you and your teams work on. You should also keep tabs on every freelancer (or have your project manager do so).

<u>Step #7:</u> Keep an eagle eye on the numbers.

As an agency owner, one of your most important jobs is to keep a close eye on your numbers — honestly, your business, and even your life, depends on them! So does the livelihood of all the people you've hired as you've grown from freelancer to agency. People are counting on you to keep them employed. If you let sales dip or decline in any way, there's more at stake than just your own income. There's nothing worse than having to let people go and reduce expenses. This lack of consistency has killed more than enough agencies.

Numbers are not just your financial earnings and expenditures, though. They also include your marketing analytics, your website traffic, your sales and leads, and anything that showcases the wealth and reach of your business.

> ➢ **Expert tip:** Software can most definitely assist with this (though you would usually have a separate application for finances and another for

marketing/sales), but also hiring a financial manager and marketing manager.

Step #8: Deliver, assess and repeat.

Once you successfully deliver those first couple of projects, you will be able to assess what systems worked best for you, how the teams performed, what problems may have cropped up, what mistakes can be avoided the next time around, and how you did overall as an agency. Assess your performance and learn from each action taken (or not taken) to keep improving your business each time you acquire a new client or undertake a new project.

Growing your own agency can be stressful at times. But it can also be one of the most exhilarating and entertaining things to do in business; you get to build a talented team, work with interesting clients, create revenue from scratch, build and brand your own small empire in whatever field you love to work in. It may be tough at times, but nothing beats having your own business.

So have some fun while you're building and growing your agency! You will work hard to get it off the ground, and you deserve to enjoy yourself every step of the way.

CONCLUSION

Congratulations for completing the journey into online business and passive income! Allow me to break down each business model one-by-one one last time to help you decide which one suits you best — not that there is any limit as to how many of these you can choose.

I'll also aim to make some connections between the various models so that you can see how one can inter-work and cross-connect with the other:

DROPSHIPPING

Dropshipping is an e-commerce business model. It an order fulfillment method wherein the business itself does not carry inventory, own a warehouse, manufacture, pack or ship orders. Instead, these tasks are performed by third-party partners.

Getting into dropshipping requires that you have some kind of passion or are somewhat excited about a particular product so that you don't give up easily when sales are low.

Benefits include low setup costs, low overhead costs and a considerably low business risk.

SELLING ON AMAZON

Selling on Amazon can be done through Amazon FBA, online arbitrage, wholesale and Amazon Private Label.

Amazon FBA is similar to dropshipping, as it is a fulfilment program for online retailers. It enables the retailer to execute customer orders without having to handle, store or ship the products sold, as Amazon takes care of all of that.

Through **Amazon online arbitrage**, you can purchase stock from either Amazon or other retailers at a lower cost, then re-sell for a higher price on the Amazon website.

With **Amazon wholesaling**, on the other hand, you would purchase your products in bulk from wholesalers, who generally sell stock at lower prices.

To stand out as a seller, you can also create your own **Amazon Private Label** business. This is the process of finding generic products that are already in demand on Amazon and developing your unique package and signature for them. It's essentially an advanced version of *Amazon FBA*.

All four of these approaches give you access to the world's largest online marketplace that is visited by over 197 million users per month!

AFFILIATE MARKETING

Affiliate marketing is the process of promoting other people's products in exchange for a small commission for each sale made.

To get started with affiliate marketing, you would have to already have a platform (website) in place before scouring affiliate websites to submit your application to join them.

NICHE WEBSITES

A **niche website** is a website dedicated to a specific topic. You can use your niche website as a gateway to your content and products, even your affiliate links and Amazon products.

Creating an **authority site** may also interest you, though it is a bigger undertaking compared to a niche website. It includes the same things as the niche website but takes it a step further in that it intends to present itself or the owner as an expert in that particular niche.

Benefits of both websites include the fact that you can host your blog, products and services on each, or at least include links to them.

SELF-PUBLISHING BOOKS

Self-published books are eBooks, print books and audiobooks you can publish on your own without the need of a traditional publishing house.

A major benefit of self-publishing is that you can earn passive income on your books for years to come. A book can function as a "business card" and proof of your expertise. It can also serve as a lead magnet to your website, email list, services or other products.

SELLING ONLINE COURSES

Selling online courses is another way to showcase your expertise and sell informational content that you would create once, yet sell for years to come. You can sell these courses via mass course platforms or through your own website.

The main benefit of selling online courses is that it is a highly sought-after passive income model during a time when an increasing amount of people are turning to online education.

FREELANCING

Freelancing is a service business model, wherein the freelancer offers their services remotely and independently. While this does include a lot of work to begin with, the freelance model is scalable, with the option to grow your services, sub-contract to other freelancers, create teams and, ultimately, build your own freelance agency.

I hope this conclusion as well as the book in its entirety has assisted you in finding the online business model that suits you the most. But this is simply the beginning of your course.

I encourage you to keep up with your research and look deeper into the online business ideas that fascinate you the most. Trends, rules, statistics and society itself are constantly changing, so you should make an effort to keep yourself – and your business – up to date with them.

And remember…learning *never* ends!

Made in the USA
Las Vegas, NV
06 February 2024

85391542R00108